becoming a man...
GOD'S WAY

a Biblical instruction manual
for true manliness & maturity

by Andrew Ash

© Copyright 2009 by Andrew Ash

All rights reserved. This book, or parts thereof, may not be reproduced in any form without permission of the author or publisher.

Scripture quotations in this book are from the King James Version of the Bible.

ISBN 978-0-578-01103-5

Published by Ash Tree Publishers, Saginaw, MI

CONTENTS

CHAPTER	TITLE	PG.
Preface		iv
Dedication		1
Chapter 1	**Manliness** - *Society's Big Misconception*	3
Chapter 2	**Love** - *The Greatest Attribute of Manliness*	9
Chapter 3	**Inner Security** - *The Unforseen Challenge*	19
Chapter 4	**Faith & Purpose** - *Where Will You End Up*	31
Chapter 5	**Purity** - *Every Man's Struggle*	39
Chapter 6	**Leadership** - *Servants Need Only to Apply*	49
Chapter 7	**Financial Stability** - *The Road Less Traveled*	57
Chapter 8	**Joyfulness** - *Always Look on the Bright Side of Life*	65
Chapter 9	**Work Ethic** - *Fundamentals for Every Day Life*	73
Chapter 10	**Communication** - *Your Thoughts Aren't Heard*	81
Conclusion		89

Preface

The Apostle Paul in writing much of the New Testament (which included lessons in spiritual growth and doctrines) once said he was the chief of sinners. You might be asking yourself, "Who is Andrew Ash and why is he worthy or knowledgeable enough to write a book on becoming a man God's way?" You're absolutely right. I'm not the chief of spiritual warriors. I'm a sinner; a sinner who wished to mature God's way and now is, and will always be, a work in progress. This book is not about me and how I've attained true manliness. It's examples and passages of God's Word put together in order to counteract the misconceptions and myths of society. I hope it is a help; for in studying it, I've learned a lot. Of course, the learning is easy. The doing is the battle.

DEDICATION

*To Pastor R. B. Ouellette and Jon Mikhail
who pointed out the immaturity in my life
and invested in me by
helping me grow spiritually.*

And

*To my wife, Marie,
who encouraged me in writing
and in editing this book.*

chapter 1

"First find the man in yourself if you will inspire manliness in others."
–Amos Bronson Alcott

Tim Allen will forever be known as Tim "the Tool Man" Taylor for his role in the TV sitcom *Home Improvement* which aired nationally from 1991 to 1999. His trademark phrases like "more power" or his neck-guttural growl at the machine that encases such power can probably be heard in the echos of your memory as you read this (if you are familiar with the show). On the show, he would introduce subjects like a bigger engine for his hotrod, a stronger man for his show, brighter Christmas lights than his neighbor's, and a garbage disposal that was so powerful it could even chip wood. How can a man not identify with Tim's views of "manliness"? His popularity skyrocketed as men (and women who know men) could identify with how most men think– bigger, better, stronger, faster. We all see it as the key traits to manliness. But what is manliness? What key ingredient changes in the life of a male from his teen years to his adult years that makes him a man and gives him the ability to exude manliness? If you ask women what that ingredient is, they'll say, "Nothing. Men never grow up. The only thing that changes is the price of their toys." This generalization may not cover every man, but if a man is honest with himself, he'll realize they are actually right. Watch a young boy play with his friends for example. He'll claim the new shoes he got will make him run faster, or the superman shirt he's wearing makes him stronger. Then, turn your gaze to a grown man. He'll claim the air filter he got for his hotrod adds three more horsepower, or the eighteen volts in his cordless drill will outlast the twelve in his neighbor's.

Everyone has a different view of manliness and thinks his view is the right one. You might imagine a muscular warrior like the man seen in the Marines commercials. One of the most recent I saw was a man fighting a big demon-like beast, and, upon conquering it, he is transformed into a soldier wearing his sharp uniform. The other was a man climbing a cliff, and when he reached the top, he then was transformed the same way. We all hold soldiers in high esteem, but maybe a muscular warrior isn't what you think manliness is all about. What about a talented athlete? The greats in recent history, like Michael Jordan, or Barry Sanders, or Wayne Gretzky were the top of the top. They could change directions while soaring through the air, outrun massive lineman and linebackers, or score more goals than anyone else while getting broadsided by a 200 pound defenseman. They are tough, graceful, and possess rare talent. The great athlete might be someone else's view of great manliness, but it might not be yours. How about a rugged hero like a police officer or fireman. There is even debate among officers and firemen over who is better. Maybe, you think of men like Clint Eastwood, John Wayne, or Harrison Ford. All of these have been idolized by society as role models of manliness. But, many times society confuses manliness with machoness.

Society feeds the male ego. Man looks at other men and covets the chief qualities, whether it be strength, courage, athleticism, possessions, and so on. We all have our specific areas that we admire. Many times, man will take these qualities and assume that women also admire and long for the same things. According to man's thinking, man admires beauty in women; therefore, women must admire it in men also. So, what do men do? They go to beauty salons trying to look "pretty" for the ladies. Men also admire strength in other men; so they work out three hours a day while downing protein shakes and popping steroids, hoping women will melt when they see them. They subscribe to a muscle magazine and try to become the man on the front cover, but women in general don't base their commitment to men by how big their deltoids are. Society knows this and tries to glamorize these faulty beliefs because they know it's what men want to hear. The result is disheartening. The wisest man ever to live noticed this. He said, "Vanity of vanities, saith the Preacher, vanity of vanities; all is vanity. What profit hath a man of all his labour which he taketh under the sun? One generation passeth away, and another generation cometh: but the earth abideth for ever" (Eccl. 1:2-4). This wise man named Solomon realized that everything man sought was vanity. There was no reward in society's view of manliness. Man worked his whole life to be great but then died, soon to be forgotten. He never found fulfillment; his greatness was overshadowed by another; his family fell apart because he was too busy excelling; he lived in slavery to debt because of the possessions he had to have; or he never felt true friendship because of his quest to better himself over his friends.

  Why does every generation of man struggle with this? The commonly quoted phrase is "Those who do not learn from the past are doomed to repeat it." Solomon said there is nothing new under the sun, but do Christian men in today's age understand that? History tells of millions of men that never listened to their forefathers. Those men destined in their own hearts that what history told them didn't apply to them, and they set out to pioneer their own trails that millions of men had already pioneered which, ultimately, led to emptiness. They blindly hurled their lives over a cliff as lemmings just because the mass herd was running that direction.

  In third grade, there was a boy that all the other boys thought was cool. He was good at sports; he always knew what to do; and he knew how to get others to "worship" him. His name was Robby, and I was under his power. One day, he decided to play in the school band, and we all followed him and his great idea. He chose to play the clarinet because he said it was cool. Coincidentally, we all began thinking the same thing, and we all signed up to play clarinet. What were we thinking???!!! As an adult, I catch myself doing the same thing. The auto makers tell me I need a new car, and I believe them. The soda company tells me I'm thirsty and to "obey [my] thirst." The exercise company tells me I'll be adored by thousands, and people won't be able to stay away from me if I use their machine thirty minutes a day, three days a week. Companies advertise the same empty rhetoric because we fall for it. Most men are followers. That's why very few men have had the descriptions "going against the grain" or "swimming against the current" or "revolutionary" assigned to them. Those few men that have had the honor of such a description are remembered for ages after.

History tells us of one Man who did not walk the path that men walked. A Man, so bold and different in His message, that thousands instantly followed Him. By His message and His life, He turned the world upside down, and there's barely a person on earth who hasn't heard of Him. His name is Jesus . . . the Perfect Man.

As a teenager, I hated hearing the phrase, "The Perfect Man." It usually left the lips of a girl in whom I was interested and was followed by the description of him or the details of the quest to find him. My buddies and I would scoff at the idea and say, "They'll never find him." In our opinion, everyone had to settle. That term usually meant a high standard set for the man they would marry. What are these standards? They were embodied in a Man that was actually perfect. He called for men to follow His teachings, and many men got so jealous of His popularity, they had Him beaten and murdered. The people never forgot Him and spread His fame worldwide.

So, what was so great about this "Perfect Man"? Since man looks on the "outward appearance," consider His stature. Most people picture the artists' renditions of Jesus Christ. Usually His body is limp; His arms are weak; and His frame appears fragile. In actuality, the paintings don't really portray His true nature; they betray it. The right perspective can be seen from an example from my teen years. I spent every summer working with my dad in construction. His expertise was in painting, and I was constantly amazed at the shape and size of his arms. He never worked-out, but he had pronounced biceps and triceps. My dad and I also had consistent contact with carpenters that were similar in size and strength. These carpenters had the luxury of power tools and pre-made materials and still had above-average strength. Jesus was a carpenter in a time when wood was cut directly from the forest by hand, floors were hewn out of stone, and walls were built of mortar not mixed by a machine. It must have been labor intensive. His body probably had more mass than the average man, and that mass was probably chiseled. He was not the effeminate man that artists made Him to be. As said before, "man looketh on the outward appearance, but the LORD looketh on the heart" (I Sam. 16:7). His strength and stature are admirable, but they weren't what made Him manly.

Greater was the attribute of His speech. The Bible sometimes uses the word *conversation* in reference to one's lifestyle. A person's speech is often a reflection of his lifestyle. Christ's speech was that of acceptance, and it conveyed love to the people. He surrounded Himself with the spiritually needy because His ministry of love called sinners to repentance. Jealous men of His time tried to trap Him in His speech, but it remained sincere and strong in the midst of their ridicule.

Not only did He have a strong stature and pleasant speech, He had a sermon that called men to be followers of Him. Chapter fifteen of John recorded a part of His message to us. He talked about abiding in Him and the importance of His love. His love was so important that He said in verse twelve, "This is my commandment, that ye love one another, as I have loved you." The "Perfect Man's" commandment to us was to be like Him and love one another. His sermon didn't hide the key traits of manliness; it called all men to learn the correct ones and follow in like manner. Are you the type of man that will heed good advice and contemplate your life, or will you try to tread your own path that millions before you have done and failed?

It's often comical and sometimes sad that man makes things harder than they actually are. We don't read instructions, ask for directions, or listen to advice. There is a group that hands out awards called "Darwin Awards" to men (and women) who prove they are not fit to survive. These men had to have done something incredibly stupid to cause their deaths, and there have been a lot of Darwin Awards given. On June 23, 2007, two men in Illinois set out to prove they were not the fittest to survive. They positioned themselves on a train track to test their reflexes by playing "chicken" with a train. The winner was Patrick Stiff. He lasted the longest, because he didn't move at all. Unbeknownst to the conductor, the train struck Patrick and continued on. I imagine Patrick probably heard at least once in his life the advice that you shouldn't play on train tracks, but he was a man that knew what he was doing.

You also have the other extreme: the overly used picture of a man that travels to the orient, climbs the steepest peak, and discovers a dwelling occupied by an old sage sitting behind a fire. The wise old man, although far removed from human contact, imparts his wisdom of the secrets of life to the exhausted seeker, who then races down the mountain to fulfill his destiny. Man, contrary to popular belief, does not have to take the hard path or make things harder than they are. There is a better way. There is an instruction manual left to man that not only tells how to be a *man*, but also gives illustrations. It was handed down to us by a Man that knew true manliness. It has lessons on key areas of manliness as lived by Jesus Christ. The following chapters point out these key areas and will help construct a Godly foundation for becoming a man . . . God's way.

love
the greatest attribute of manliness

chapter 2

*"Greater love hath no man than this,
that a man lay down his life for his friends."*
–Jesus Christ

What defines man? Many will say that a man's legacy defines him such as what he leaves behind, what great accomplishment he performed, or how many people know who he was. One such man that accomplished something great was Charles "Chuck" Yeager. On October 14, 1947, he stepped into the Bell X-1 aircraft. The plane was practically a seat inside a rocket. This dangerous machine was strapped to the bottom of a B-29 bomber. The B-29 dropped the airplane, and the ignition on the X-1 was hit. For the first time in history, man traveled faster than the speed of sound. He was the only man ever to have broken the sound barrier. Shortly after, another did it, and another, and another. There has been thousands since. So what? He conquered the unconquerable, and now man does it on a daily basis. You can pick the accomplishment, and there will be somebody to do it faster, stronger, higher, longer, etc. Just watch the Olympics. Someone breaks a record almost every Olympic season. Great accomplishments are achieved, and people hope their accomplishment doesn't get surpassed. Jesus Christ conquered the unconquerable, and He doesn't say, "I'm gonna be the only one ever to do this"; He tells us to do it just as He did. Not many people know who Chuck Yeager is. Most people can't tell you what Willie Mayes or Sir Edmund Hillary or Amerigo Vespucci did. But most people can tell you what Jesus Christ did. Jesus Christ's accomplishment turned the world upside down. How did he do it? He did it by true love.

Matthew 22:36-38 tells the story of a Pharisee asking Jesus the question, "Which is the great commandment in the law?" He replied, "Thou shalt love the Lord thy God with all thy heart, and with all thy soul, and with all thy mind. This is the first and great commandment. And the second is like unto it, Thou shalt love thy neighbour as thyself. On these two commandments hang all the law and the prophets." The foundation of the whole Bible is a pair of commandments to love. The Bible is often referred to as God's love letter to us.

So what is love? I had a secular job in which a co-worker stood up one day and gave his belief on love. He began to tell of a scientific finding that said that love was a sensual, chemical reaction in the body that was only produced for a span of three years in a man. This dated back to the primal days when a man would mate, help raise the child till about two, then leave the woman for another. He wholeheartedly believed that love was a feeling that lasted for three years. Society has some strange views on love, but the ancient Greeks differentiated between the types of love. Their language split love into three basic types.

The first is the *eros* (ερος) love. This is the "love" on which society focuses. We get our modern day English word *erotic* from it. It is purely physical and is the term to which my coworker was referring. You will not find this Greek word anywhere in the Bible. It's main characteristic is a short-lived physical satisfaction. It can be compared to a drug. The user dabbles in it till he is calloused, then he has to look for something greater to appease his physical satisfaction. Then, when that is calloused, he has to go farther and farther. Sometimes, this type of love does not turn out to be the fulfillment one thought it would be. Take for example a story about King David's family found in II Samuel 13. David's son Amnon loved his half-sister. The Hebrew word for love that is used is a sexual attraction toward someone. He acted on his friend's plan to rape her, and after he had fulfilled his desires with her, the Bible records the outcome in this sad verse: "Then Amnon hated her exceedingly; so that the hatred wherewith he hated her was greater than the love wherewith he had loved her. And Amnon said unto her, Arise, be gone." He gave in to the erotic love and found that it didn't fulfill him. *Eros* has the strongest feelings of the three types of love which makes it very hard for man to control.

The second love found in the Greek language is *phileo* (φιλέω). This love can be described as a friendship love. It can be between a man and a man or a man and a woman or a woman and a woman and not change meaning. It brings comfort to relationship as it understands differences in the other but invests in the similarities. Two people build knowledge about each other with this love.

The third and most important love is *agape* (αγαπη). This is a giving love. It doesn't seek getting. It doesn't perform an action to get something in return. It gives unconditionally. There's a story told in the Old Testament about a man named Hosea. God used him as an example to the Israelites to show what Israel had done. He told Hosea to take a wife who would bear him children. Hosea did what God said and after she bore him children, she left him and committed adultery as a harlot. She became a slave, and God told Hosea to buy her back. Even though she didn't love him, Hosea loved her. Far greater than the story of Hosea is the example of Christ. Imagine the magnitude of His sacrifice. He created man much like a man would create a pot. Man chose to deny Him and follow other gods. God loved man so much that He became his own creation; let his creation reject Him again; let his creation torture Him; and then let His creation crucify Him so that He could pay for His creation's sins and allow them to go to Heaven. He expressed the importance of this love in John 15:12-13: "This is my commandment, That ye love one another, as I have loved you. Greater love hath no man than this, that a man lay down his life for his friends." This love he spoke of was the agape one. A giving love that finds its ultimate definition in sacrifice. So, how does this correlate with maturing and manliness?

Paul explains this type of love and ties it in with maturity in I Corinthians 13. The English translators described *agape* here as *charity*, which, of course, fits very well. It is a giving from the heart. As you read this passage, take note to verse 11:

> 1) Though I speak with the tongues of men and of angels, and have not <u>charity</u>, I am become as sounding brass, or a tinkling cymbal.
> 2) And though I have the gift of prophecy, and understand all mysteries, and all knowledge; and though I have all faith, so that I could remove mountains, and have not <u>charity</u>, I am nothing.
> 3) And though I bestow all my goods to feed the poor, and though I give my body to be burned, and have not <u>charity</u>, it profiteth me nothing.
> 4) <u>Charity</u> suffereth long, and is kind; <u>charity</u> envieth not; <u>charity</u> vaunteth not itself, is not puffed up,
> 5) Doth not behave itself unseemly, seeketh not her own, is not easily provoked, thinketh no evil;
> 6) Rejoiceth not in iniquity, but rejoiceth in the truth;
> 7) Beareth all things, believeth all things, hopeth all things, endureth all things.
> 8) <u>Charity</u> never faileth: but whether there be prophecies, they shall fail; whether there be tongues, they shall cease; whether there be knowledge, it shall vanish away.
> 9) For we know in part, and we prophesy in part.
> 10) But when that which is perfect is come, then that which is in part shall be done away.
> 11) <u>When I was a child, I spake as a child, I understood as a child, I thought as a child: but when I became a man, I put away childish things.</u>
> 12) For now we see through a glass, darkly; but then face to face: now I know in part; but then shall I know even as also I am known.
> 13) And now abideth faith, hope, charity, these three; but the greatest of these is charity.

People often overlook verse eleven and don't connect it with the rest of the passage, but it is an important part of the passage. The apostle Paul was talking about how great a giving love is in Christianity. He draws a strong comparison of love to what we think is great. If a man were to come into a church and just start speaking in every known language and then speak in a language we knew as the angels' language, we would be in awe. If he came to the church and started telling the future accurately, then told you all the answers to man's mysteries, then took you outside and with his voice moved a mountain by faith, you would be in awe of him. Paul says that none of those great attributes can compare to having a love that gives. Paul then throws in verse eleven which cannot be separated from the passage. His statement is that all the things man thinks are so great are childlike ambitions and admirations that cannot compare to a mature man's attribute of a giving love. He put away his admirations and his quest of becoming great to become a mature man that loves. In other words, love is the greatest attribute a mature man can have.

    Paul's description of love is even more detailed than giving. He breaks love down and attacks many of the areas that men call manliness. He says that love is patient. It doesn't seek to push the other in a relationship faster than they want to go or should go. Such pushes could include immorality, finances, marriage, etc. But this love isn't just focused on relationships. It includes your attitude toward society and individuals you don't even know. Consider the simple action of driving a car. When I was young, I saw a Disney cartoon that starred Goofy. He was portrayed as a family man who was kind. He kissed his wife and hugged his son as he left for work. It was a cheerful scene. Waiving to his family, he backed out of his driveway and headed down the street. His happy demeanor took a 180° turn, and pretty soon he was screaming at people and driving on the sidewalk. His road rage made him the opposite of what you thought him to be. Although it was a cartoon, it's not far from the truth. I caught myself getting upset at a woman in oncoming traffic one day. She was making a right turn, and I was making a left. She motioned for me to go ahead with my turn. How stupid could she be??!! She was wasting time!!! "Just go," I thought. Doesn't she know she has the right-of-way? Regardless, I got upset in an instant, and at what? She was showing me courtesy. If I had followed Paul's definition, I would have been patient with her even though

I didn't know her. Patience is just one attribute of love.

Another attribute of love is kindness. But, again, love mentioned here is not just in reference to a personal relationship. Love doesn't demean people or put them down, no matter who they are. As a teenager, I remember sitting in class one day as a female teacher was teaching. There were two guys in the class that made their thoughts vocal about the teacher at her expense. On one occasion, the teacher asked if one of the guys could help her as she tried to adjust the lectern. His response was, "I'm not a psychiatrist." On another occasion, the two boys were acting up in class. The teacher said, "Boys . . ." To which they corrected her and said, "Men . . ." She said, "I'll call you *men*, when you start acting like one." One of them responded, "Can we call you what you act like?" and they began to make horse whinny sounds. Although these quick responses were harsh, I couldn't help but chuckle inside. Their sharp and cruel mind was astonishing to me. It was a funny response to the listeners, but not to her. She began to cry and left the room. I felt for her, but didn't understand the magnitude of what she was going through until later in life. After I graduated college, I taught high school for two years and realized the pain a teacher goes through as they work night and day and invest so much in their students, only to have apathy and disdain in return. It tore me up inside. If those two *boys* only knew how to love, they wouldn't have bitten the hand that fed them.

How can love envy either? Envy is often confused with jealousy, but it's much worse. It doesn't just wish it had something the other person has, it wants it so badly it wishes the other person didn't have it. We often deceive ourselves and think we don't envy, but imagine a neighbor of yours one day gets a Ferrari 355 Spyder. Every sunny day, he pulls it out of his garage and sits in the driveway revving the smooth, purring engine. He passes your house at a high speed and gives you a look of "Don't you wish you had one?" You watch him go by, and you chuckle to yourself as you think of that pristine vehicle sitting under a pile of manure with him in it. Yet, on the outside, you play it off and wave. Is this thought a love that bypasses insecurity and rejoices in your neighbor's good fortune? Real love doesn't envy.

Love doesn't lift one's self up either. It isn't self-centered. This attribute has been a thorn in my side for years. I struggle with being a people pleaser. I used to look for approval from my parents the most. I remember playing a football game in college where I caught a 65 yard pass and had an interception in front of hundreds of high school students, college students, and adults. I scanned the crowd throughout the game and never saw my parents. I came home and let loose on them for not being at a game which was important to me. I went into my bedroom and cried myself to sleep. I was twenty years old. I was a grown man, and I wept like a baby because my parents didn't see me play. The ultimate reason I wanted them to be there–so they could see how good I was and praise me. A few years later, my pastor at the church for which I work saw this immature trait in me and tried to help me with it, but I didn't understand. I didn't think I was *trying* to get people to like me and think I'm great. He told me to memorize Psalm 139 (which will be covered in depth in a later chapter). I didn't get the chapter completely memorized, but I read it several times, and one day while reading the book, *How to Win Friends and Influence People* by Dale Carnegie, it all clicked. People don't care how much you know until they know how much you care. It was soon after, that I met my wife. She will say now that I was so different than most guys she had met because in our first conversation, I kept asking her questions about herself and what she thought about things. My focus wasn't on me and how great I thought I was. It was on her. Love is not self-centered.

Love doesn't act in an unacceptable fashion. It finds its actions as proper and never strange. Oxford University Press says the word pervert means "**verb 1** alter from an original meaning or state to a corruption of what was first intended. **2** lead away from what is right, natural, or acceptable. >**noun** a person with abnormal or unacceptable sexual behavior." Love does not claim it is love and then do something contrary to it. That is a perversion. Love only does that which is acceptable. For

15

example, love gives to the homosexual, but does not partake in his sin. It gives the woman her purity and does not take a woman in lust and call it love.

In the mid '90s, a high school freshman named Mike visited a church youth group meeting while not knowing anyone there. The youth pastor had this crazy idea that teens should get out of their comfort zones and befriend new people. He had the teens find someone they didn't know and ask them who they were, how old they were, and the type of deodorant they used. Two older guys found Mike and welcomed him. These guys didn't go to a public school like Mike. They didn't share his great admiration for golf the way he did. They didn't even have an upbringing or family structure like his. They did, however, step away from their selfishness to make this visitor welcome. It's not that much of an accomplishment, but the small amount of love expressed in that little time led Mike to join the church, go to Bible college, meet and marry a wonderful girl, and then become a youth pastor. He now extends that love to other teens. Love that extends past similarities, or race, or gender, or whatever the differences, is rare, but it is powerful. A man with true love doesn't seek after others just like himself; he reaches out and accepts others regardless of the differences. When following this attribute, you won't have a problem with the next trait of love.

Love is not easily provoked. Ask yourself the following questions: Do you ever fly off the handle, let your blood pressure rise, or forget to count to ten? What about pet peeves? Have any of those? Have any thing that jerks your chain, riles you up, busts your bubble, or raws your hide? If a person can push your buttons and make you explode, it might be due to a lack of love, because love is not easily provoked, neither does it think evil. As said before, accepting people where they are is a true state of love. God made us all different, and we all have differing beliefs. Love looks beyond the differences and sees a soul stricken with the sins of this world.

So, what if you are easy going and not easily provoked? Maybe that's not you. Do you ever laugh at sin or rejoice in it? Before you answer that question, think about someone in folklore. His story has been handed down to each generation. Millions know his name and cheered his efforts. His name is Robinhood. He was a thief, and we've rooted for him in movies. Hollywood has adopted this and has easily lured people into rejoicing in sin. We've stood on the side of a warrior who is fighting for revenge, or hoped for a wife who kills an abusive husband, or laughed at an actor telling dirty jokes, or watched a so-called "married couple" sleeping together while we entertain the thought that it's okay because they are married. These ideologies are wrong. Revenge is from God. Murder is not an exit for an abusive marriage. Comedy isn't an excuse to curse. And actors playing married people doesn't make them married. Even if they were, it doesn't make it right for others to watch. Our society is calloused and is constantly rejoicing in sin. Love desires purity and sanctification. It doesn't rejoice in sin. Love rejoices in the truth. It hopes and believes the best in people.

  These are the attributes of a mature man. Everything in life will fail, but real love will never fail. Christ set the example. You might be athletic; you might be strong; your might have good looks; you might have money or possessions; but, according to God, if you don't have love, you are nothing.

inner security
the unforeseen challenge

chapter 3

*"He who is humble is confident and wise.
He who brags is insecure and lacking."*
–Lisa Edmondson

Have you ever heard the phrase "If you look good, you feel good"? Why does looking good make you feel good? You can't see yourself. You left the mirror five minutes ago. What if something has changed in your appearance since then? That memory of you standing in front of the mirror sticks with you, and deep down you know that others see you in that state. It's true that we all long for the acceptance of our peers. Some people focus their lives around that acceptance, but what they fail to realize is that when they get caught up in the quest to make other people like or accept them, they end up turning people away.

So, the question is "How secure do you gauge yourself?" Do you think you are secure? Are you comfortable with who you are? Well then, I dare you to take this little six-question test, and I dare you to be brutally honest with yourself:

1. Have you recently bought anything (i.e. clothing, vehicle, sporting

equipment, etc) with the thought that someone will be impressed with you or that your popularity will improve?

2. Have you recently performed an action, whether it be sports, construction, music, etc., to gain praise or recognition from someone?

3. Have you recently said something smart, eloquent, or braggadocios to someone to show how smart, smooth, or adept you are?

4. Have you recently blown-up on someone?

5. Have you recently defended yourself against teasing?

6. Have you recently taken an insecurity test to prove to the author (and yourself) that you aren't insecure?

If you've answered yes to any of the questions above, you might have a problem with insecurity. You aren't alone. It is very prevalent in our society. It has to be battled on a daily basis because everything around you attacks your insecurity. Just watch five minutes of commercials. You'll be subtly attacked numerous times. Combating this insecurity is one of the great steps to maturing God's way. Once you realize that you're insecure, you'll be amazed at how quickly you notice the traits. The two major manifestations of insecurity are lack of meekness and lack of confidence.

Don't get turned away by the word meekness. It might not be what you think it is. Society has often defined meekness as weakness or timidness. Their philosophy says that if you've got it, flaunt it. They might even convince you that if you have a good reason, such as revenge, it's ok to go on a rampage. Although this flaunting and exploding feels good, it doesn't fulfill your needs or anyone else's. Christ knew the hearts of men and encouraged them in Matthew 5:5, "Blessed are the meek: for they shall inherit the earth." As mentioned before, Christ was in no way weak. So if meekness is not weakness, what is it? Easton's 1897 Bible Dictionary says it is "a calm temper of mind, not easily provoked." My youth pastor, summed it up in three simple words–"Power under control."

Imagine for a moment that you're going into battle. On the table in front of you, you have two normal looking H&K MP5 submachine guns, with each clip holding 30 rounds. They are high-quality guns that are trusted by special forces around the world. The one on the left is known to be accurate. It has single shot, 3-round burst, and fully automatic capabilities. The safety is in perfect working condition and the trigger has a well-adjusted pull. The gun on the right looks just like the one on the left, but it has a slight defect. Periodically, the gun on the right fires without warning. It likes to "show off" or "blow up." You could be sneaking around the battlefield looking for the enemy, and the gun will go off and give away your position or, in a more severe case, accidentally kill a friendly soldier. The gun has explosive, raw power, but it's dangerous and scary. Anyone in their right mind would pick the gun on the left that has its power under control.

Now liken yourself to those guns. Which one are you? When someone begins to tell a story, are you eager for them to finish so you can interject your story or tell them of something better? Maybe you have to enlighten others on the subject of your great abilities or accomplishments. What about getting upset at small matters? You might have great accomplishments or abilities, but do you have them under control? You'll find that people are observant; you don't need to tell others about your abilities. People look at guns with a fear and reverence to the awesome power they can wield. They don't have to be told how powerful a gun is, they know it by its actions. Lord Chesterfield said, "Never seem wiser, nor more learned, than the people you are with. Wear your learning like your watch, in a private pocket: don't pull it out to count the minutes; pull it out to give the time when asked."

To pay my way through college, I worked as a medical dispatcher at an ambulance company in California. It was an interesting job with all types of employees. One such person was my night supervisor who was an ex-marine sniper. He was a barrel-chested man that carried himself abrasively. He walked around with a chip on his shoulder and was ready to give a condescending look to anyone he deemed worthy. I thought very highly of the position he once held. He had exciting stories of kills he had made that had since been declassified, but there was something I didn't like about him. I didn't like being around him for long periods of time. I felt like I had to walk on egg shells, so he wouldn't judge me or look down on me for something I said. People feared him not because he could snap their neck in less than a second but because his power was not under control. He flaunted his superiority around people, and people did not like it.

Lack of control is a dangerous trait as seen in James 3:2-8:

2 For in many things we offend all. If any man offend not in word, the same is a perfect man, and able also to bridle the whole body.
3 Behold, we put bits in the horses' mouths, that they may obey us; and we turn about their whole body.
4 Behold also the ships, which though they be so great, and are driven of fierce winds, yet are they turned about with a very small helm, whithersoever the governor listeth.
5 Even so the tongue is a little member, and boasteth great things. Behold, how great a matter a little fire kindleth!
6 And the tongue is a fire, a world of iniquity: so is the tongue among our members, that it defileth the whole body, and setteth on fire the course of nature; and it is set on fire of hell.
7 For every kind of beasts, and of birds, and of serpents, and of things in the sea, is tamed, and hath been tamed of mankind:
8 But the tongue can no man tame; it is an unruly evil, full of deadly poison.

The tongue is such a powerful object. A man that can control his tongue is a perfect man and also able to control his own body. No man can tame the tongue. The Bible talks of a beautiful angel that also had a problem controlling his tongue. He was not able to keep his power under control. Ezekiel 28:12-19 says:

12 Son of man, take up a lamentation upon the king of Tyrus, and say unto him, Thus saith the Lord GOD; Thou sealest up the sum, full of wisdom, and perfect in beauty.
13 Thou hast been in Eden the garden of God; every precious stone was thy covering, the sardius, topaz, and the diamond, the beryl, the onyx, and the jasper, the sapphire, the emerald, and the carbuncle, and gold: the

workmanship of thy tabrets and of thy pipes was prepared in thee in the day that thou wast created.
14 Thou art the anointed cherub that covereth; and I have set thee so: thou wast upon the holy mountain of God; thou hast walked up and down in the midst of the stones of fire.
15 Thou wast perfect in thy ways from the day that thou wast created, till iniquity was found in thee.
16 By the multitude of thy merchandise they have filled the midst of thee with violence, and thou hast sinned: therefore I will cast thee as profane out of the mountain of God: and I will destroy thee, O covering cherub, from the midst of the stones of fire.
17 Thine heart was lifted up because of thy beauty, thou hast corrupted thy wisdom by reason of thy brightness: I will cast thee to the ground, I will lay thee before kings, that they may behold thee.
18 Thou hast defiled thy sanctuaries by the multitude of thine iniquities, by the iniquity of thy traffick; therefore will I bring forth a fire from the midst of thee, it shall devour thee, and I will bring thee to ashes upon the earth in the sight of all them that behold thee.
19 All they that know thee among the people shall be astonished at thee: thou shalt be a terror, and never shalt thou be any more.

    Lucifer held one of the highest positions in the angel hierarchy. He stood over God's throne and spread his wings over it. You could imagine God's bright glory shining through those precious stones and getting refracted all over Heaven like a prism refracts light. Even after God left his presence, Lucifer probably still glowed and shone forth just like Moses did after returning from God's presence. He saw himself and his beauty and deceived himself and thought himself to be great. He had no humility and now his future is doomed. Paul said in Romans 7:18, "For I know that in me (that is, in my flesh) dwelleth no good thing."

    Let me tell you about an ex-marine sniper I knew. No, you're not having déjà vu. This is a different ex-marine sniper. I met this man when he became the teacher of my college and career Sunday school class. The man was large, but he handled himself with a genuine and soft spirit. When he would get up and speak of the amazing character of God, he would get choked up and begin to cry. The man truly cared about others. It wasn't until about a year after knowing this pleasant man that I discovered he had been a marine sniper. He was soft and genuine, but he could also snap your neck in less than a second. He never said a word about his ability. I was astonished. How can you have such a proud background and not mention it? He realized the important things in life were not his abilities, but God's goodness. People loved to be around him and his joy. I admired him greatly for his ability, but far more for his character. He was truly a meek man.

A greater example of meekness is found in Philippians 2:6-8, "Who, being in the form of God, thought it not robbery to be equal with God: But made himself of no reputation, and took upon him the form of a servant, and was made in the likeness of men: And being found in fashion as a man, he humbled himself, and became obedient unto death, even the death of the cross." There is no greater example of meekness than a perfect, all-powerful being becoming His creation and letting His creation kill Him. He could have spoken and had every man on earth eradicated, but He kept his power under control.

Meekness has many benefits. Matthew 5:5 says the meek will "inherit the earth." Matthew 11:29 says the meek and lowly in heart have "rest in their souls." Do you know anybody that lacks rest because of a lack of meekness? I have a family member who fights for what she believe they deserve. They throw their weight around to get what they want. It seems like her life is one long battle. There's no peace in her life. The things they fight for doesn't make them happy. It just alienates the people with whom they fight. Another benefit can be illustrated by a picture of two dogs. One dog is snarling and growling, and the other is wagging its tail. Which would you approach? Obviously the friendly dog! Meekness results in an inviting personality. The friendly dog can bite your hand, but it chooses to lick it instead. Do you have power under control?

Although you may not have blown up on someone, have you ever struggled with confidence? Have you ever relied on yourself, your abilities, or some piece of property to produce confidence? Society tells you that that's the way you get it. Commercials constantly tell you that you have to have something external to make you feel normal. Society tells you that what you wear gives you a status and people judge you on how you look. Society tells you that you have to have the newest and brightest car to make you feel good about yourself. You can watch a minute of commercials and be bombarded with subtle hints that they can fix your insecurity. They present a rugged cowboy smoking a cigarette with a beautiful woman by his side and claims you will be accepted if you buy their cigarettes. Do you remember dressing up in a costume when you were little? I can remember having a Superman outfit when I was five years old. I watched superman on TV, and when he wore his outfit, his muscles bulged through the suit. I would don the suit, look in the mirror, and for some reason, it didn't quite look like the hero I just recently beheld. The pants were so loose, and I was so small that I could take two steps in them before they moved. The top was also loose revealing that I had absolutely no muscles at all. Maybe I was missing something. I had gotten the hair down–that was easy. Aha! I was missing two items. How could I forget the red underwear on the outside of the pants and the red boots. As a five-year-old, I didn't have red underwear, but I did have white Superman underwear and yellow galoshes. I quickly remedied my deficiencies, but I still was left wanting. What was up? My parents forked out the money for the costume, but I was still the same little kid inside. Without knowing it, we, yes, *we* get fooled by society constantly. We think the external things or the flaunting of our abilities is going to give us confidence, but they don't. We're still the same person inside. It's like the heavy-set woman wearing spandex. It's not going to make her lighter. Companies see you as a dollar signs. They don't want you to be secure. They want you to think you can't live without their product. Their product that will make you accepted by everyone.

Luke 15:11-15 talks of one who had a false sense of fulfillment:

11 And he said, A certain man had two sons:
12 And the younger of them said to his father, Father, give me the portion of goods that falleth to me. And he divided unto them his living.
13 And not many days after the younger son gathered all together, and took his journey into a far country, and there wasted his substance with riotous living.

14 And when he had spent all, there arose a mighty famine in that land; and he began to be in want.
15 And he went and joined himself to a citizen of that country; and he sent him into his fields to feed swine.

He wasted his money with riotous living. Where were his friends when his money ran out? Where were the companies with whom he bought items when his money ran out? Where was his security? He was eating with the pigs. Society gives you a false sense of confidence. It can never fulfill you. Solomon said in Ecclesiastes 1:1-3, "The words of the Preacher, the son of David, king in Jerusalem. Vanity of vanities, saith the Preacher, vanity of vanities; all is vanity. What profit hath a man of all his labour which he taketh under the sun?" Man hasn't changed. He still looks for confidence in all the wrong places.

On a PBS program, Daniel Boorstin, once the Librarian of Congress, brought out a small blue box from a closet that held the library's rarities. On the box, you could read the label: "Contents of the President's pockets on the night of April 14, 1865." If you know your history, you can identify that date as the day Abraham Lincoln was assassinated. The little blue box was then opened and revealed a handkerchief, a glasses case, a pen knife, a money purse, and some old and worn newspaper clippings. Everything made sense with the exception of the newspaper clippings. Boorstin said, "The clippings were concerned with the great deeds of Abraham Lincoln, and one of them actually reports a speech by John Bright which says that Abraham Lincoln is 'one of the greatest men of all times.'" That wasn't a popular belief about Lincoln at the time. He had a lot of critics which made his lot in life a lonely one in a time when the country was torn apart by civil war. A little quote on a tattered piece of paper was reviewed often by one of the greatest Presidents of the U.S. to build his confidence. The article was written by a simple journalist, but it meant the world to a President. We have a far greater compliment than the one bestowed on President Lincoln. God tells us what He thinks about us in Psalm 139.

GOD KNOWS MORE ABOUT YOU THAN YOU DO.

1 O LORD, thou hast searched me, and known me.
2 Thou knowest my downsitting and mine uprising, thou understandest my thought afar off.
3 Thou compassest my path and my lying down, and art acquainted with all my ways.
4 For there is not a word in my tongue, but, lo, O LORD, thou knowest it altogether.
5 Thou hast beset me behind and before, and laid thine hand upon me.
6 Such knowledge is too wonderful for me; it is high, I cannot attain unto it.
7 Whither shall I go from thy spirit? or whither shall I flee from thy presence?
8 If I ascend up into heaven, thou art there: if I make my bed in hell, behold, thou art there.

My greatest aspiration as a teenager was to go to the Air Force Academy, join flight training, and fly fighter jets. I had practically everything I needed–the GPA, the recommendations, the extra curricular, etc., but one day I didn't feel right about the decision I had made. I prayed and asked God what He wanted, and after a lengthy battle of wills, I surrendered mine. I was heart-broken. My dreams faded away like steam above a boiling pot, but I knew God knew what was best. I went to Bible college and got a job at Edwards Air Force Base during one of the summer breaks. It was a great job that put me around airplanes constantly. I talked with pilots and engineers and practically saw the whole base with my security clearance. By the end of the summer, I was sure of one thing–I'm glad I didn't become a pilot. The novelty and excitement of it wore off. God knew me better than I knew myself.

GOD WILL ALWAYS BE THERE FOR US.

7 Whither shall I go from thy spirit? or whither shall I flee from thy presence?
8 If I ascend up into heaven, thou art there: if I make my bed in hell, behold, thou art there.
9 If I take the wings of the morning, and dwell in the uttermost parts of the sea;
10 Even there shall thy hand lead me, and thy right hand shall hold me.
11 If I say, Surely the darkness shall cover me; even the night shall be light about me.
12 Yea, the darkness hideth not from thee; but the night shineth as the day: the

darkness and the light are both alike to thee.
13 For thou hast possessed my reins: thou hast covered me in my mother's womb.

If you've ever left home for an extended period of time, you know what it's like to miss home and miss a friendly face. God will be there for us even when the world abandons us. You can always go to God with your burdens.

GOD MADE US IN HIS PERFECTION.

14 I will praise thee; for I am fearfully and wonderfully made: marvellous are thy works; and that my soul knoweth right well.
15 My substance was not hid from thee, when I was made in secret, and curiously wrought in the lowest parts of the earth.
16 Thine eyes did see my substance, yet being unperfect; and in thy book all my members were written, which in continuance were fashioned, when as yet there was none of them.

When God made you, He was perfect. He made you exactly the way He wanted. He knows every little detail about you. He made you different than everyone else because He wanted you to be unique. Could you imagine going to your closet and every outfit you owned was a suit? You had to swim in a suit, work on your car in a suit, lounge around the house in a suit. What about your tools? You go to your workbench and all you have are slotted screw drivers. Good luck getting through that 2x4 you have to cut with only a slotted screw driver. Society wants to make you a clone of someone else. God made you just the way you are because your differences make you interesting.

GOD THINKS ABOUT US MORE THAN ANY HUMAN.

17 How precious also are thy thoughts unto me, O God! how great is the sum of them!
18 If I should count them, they are more in number than the sand: when I awake, I am still with thee.

His thoughts are greater than the sand of the sea. He has had more thought about your situation, than anyone else has. Have you ever gone to someone and told them a trouble you had? I have and have gotten two different answers. The first is a quick answer–the result of someone's opinion. The second is a wise answer that goes something like this, "Let me pray about it, and I'll get back to you." Which do you think is better? The opinion that took barely any thought into your situation, or the access to a God who has thought about it more than you? God knows our trials and struggles and thinks about us. We can have confidence in His thoughts and decisions.

GOD WILL TAKE CARE OF YOUR ENEMIES.
19 Surely thou wilt slay the wicked, O God: depart from me therefore, ye bloody men.
20 For they speak against thee wickedly, and thine enemies take thy name in vain.
21 Do not I hate them, O LORD, that hate thee? and am not I grieved with those that rise up against thee?
22 I hate them with perfect hatred: I count them mine enemies.

Besides working at the church, God has generously provided me with a good job as an emergency dispatcher at 9-1-1. Occasionally we'll get someone calling who is in the middle of yelling at someone they don't like. The caller doesn't listen to a thing the dispatcher is asking because they are yelling at someone else. When we're finally able to get their attention, we try to get them to realize that no matter how much they yell at the person, they are not just going to stop and say, "You're right! I never saw it that way. I didn't know you felt that way. I'm going to change right now. I'm sorry." As ridiculous as this sounds, we often worry about what our enemies think about us. Put your confidence in God, and He'll take care of your enemies.

GOD TRULY WANTS WHAT'S BEST FOR YOU.
23 Search me, O God, and know my heart: try me, and know my thoughts:
24 And see if there be any wicked way in me, and lead me in the way everlasting.

Society doesn't care about you. They just care about your pocket book. They don't care if you go in debt to pay for the item that's supposed to make you popular. God knows what is best for you, and you can find your confidence in Him.

Whether you have a lack of meekness or a lack of confidence, God's love and example can help cultivate inner security by helping you trust in Him. Society leaves you wanting more; God fulfills you with how He made you. Society will accept you one day and reject you the next; God will always be there. Society will always provide enemies; God promises to take care of your enemies (Prov. 16:7). When you understand God's thoughts about you, you can handle anything with inner security.

chapter 4

"He who chooses the beginning of a road chooses the place it leads to. It is the means that determine the end."
–H.E. Fosdick

Where is your road leading you? Every decision brings you to follow a specific road that leads to a specific end. You might start on a path and think that the outcome isn't that bad, but will you still think that when you get to the end of the road? For example, you might not think that sexual immorality is that bad, but one day, if you follow that path, you might find you have a lack of self respect, a sexually transmitted disease, or an unwanted child. Are you going to think you made the right decision then? Some people don't care what the outcome of their choices is because they think their decisions only affect them.

On May 5, 1818, a boy was born in Trier, Prussia. He was the third child of seven. His father, Herchel Mordechai, was a Jewish Lawyer who descended from a long line of rabbis. One day, the Prussian authorities told Herchel that he could not practice law as a Jew, so he joined the Lutheran church which was the denomination of the Prussian state. His son witnessed this and stored it away in his memory. The boy grew up and attended the University of Bonn in 1835, where he became the president of the Trier Tavern Club Drinking Society. He then transferred to Friedrich-Wilhelms-Universitat in Berlin. While there, he acquired the atheistic views of the Young Hegelians. He became anti-semetic and criticized people of religion. He said that religion was just a "sigh of the oppressed creature, the heart of a heartless world, and the soul of soulless conditions. It is the opium of the people." He equated religion to a drug that makes people feel good. He formulated his governmental views that were published abroad. Governments around the world have been inundated with his ideas. You may have heard of him. His name is Karl Marx, the man accredited with basic concepts of communism. The Bolshevik Revolution was fought because people believed in his ideas. Countries have seen decay and poverty and religions were oppressed because of his beliefs. Marx's father chose a path to betray his own religion. His father led him in an example that he took to the next step. Herchel made one decision that seemed insignificant in the world's perspective at the time, but his son Karl witnessed it and took it a step further. Every decision you make will have a consequence. It might be very small, or it might be one that changes the world.

Even though you may think your position in life is not one of influence, it is. What path have you chosen for your life? Proverbs 29:18 says, "Where there is no vision, the people perish . . ." If you don't have a purpose for your life, you'll perish. To escape the fate of a dead life, you need to find real purpose. The world has many faulty purposes. One purpose might be to make money. Did you ever see the bumper sticker that says, "He who dies with the most toys wins"? Wins what? The logic was disputed by the other bumper sticker that says, "He who dies with the most toys still dies." It's like the wealthy old man that told his wife he wanted all his money buried with him when he died. He passed away and pretty soon, she was on a shopping spree. One of his friends who heard his dying wish confronted her about it. She quickly answered her accuser and said, "He's buried with his money. I wrote him a check. It's not my fault if he can't cash it." An accumulation of possessions won't fulfill your need for purpose. It will always leave you wanting more.

Another purpose of the world might be to just have fun in life. Commercials and TV shows show people having a good time drinking, smoking, going to wild parties, and doing everything imaginable. Unfortunately, they don't show the outcome. They don't show the shallow relationships, the angry drunk or the sick drunk; they don't show you the emphysema or lung cancer; they don't show the doctor's office when someone is told they have an STD; and they don't show the police officer and the chaplain going to a relative's house to break the bad news of an early death. Maybe it's not that serious of a desire to have fun. Maybe you just want to play video games or goof-off and not study or serve God. You might one day look back and regret it. More and more adults are going back to college in their middle age because they made poor decisions in their young age.

If you follow the purposes of the world, not only will it ruin your life, it will affect those around you and after you. Your friends won't really be true friends, your relationships will wither because they are based on the world's ideas, and your quest for possessions that really didn't please you continually will bring you debt and work for years on end. Earlier we saw the first half of Proverbs 29:18. The second half of the verse says, "but he that keepeth the law, happy is he." I was born in 1980. My first memory didn't come until I was a baby lying in my crib. I have a few memories from my terrible two's, but I didn't start to rationally think until 4. That gives me about a quarter of a century of learning and thinking that I can remember. I can't tell you how my brain works, how memories are stored, or even how my emotions work. I can tell you that God has been around before this world began. I can tell you that Psalm 139 says He knows everything about me. If God has been around that long and knows everything about me, why on earth would I want to trust my purpose-driven life instead of His?

When God gives you a purpose, you will never be unhappy. There is peace, fulfillment, and excitement in trusting God. You have the peace of knowing you're doing what's right. You have fulfillment in knowing you have a good reason for living, and when you trust God and He answers prayer and provides for you, it is the most amazing experience that cannot be described in words. So what is God's purpose for you? Romans 15:4-6 says, "For whatsoever things were written aforetime were written for our learning, that we through patience and comfort of the scriptures might have hope. Now the God of patience and consolation grant you to be likeminded one toward another according to Christ Jesus: That ye may with one mind and one mouth glorify God, even the Father of our Lord Jesus Christ." God made us to glorify Him. We represent Christ. We were created in the image of God, in His likeness. That's an awesome responsibility.

Another purpose is to invest in eternity. Matthew 6:19-20 states, "Lay not up for yourselves treasures upon earth, where moth and rust doth corrupt, and where thieves break through and steal: But lay up for yourselves treasures in heaven, where neither moth nor rust doth corrupt, and where thieves do not break through nor steal:" If you have ever invested money in mutual funds or the stock market, you will see only temporary returns. It might be a great increase in wealth, but one day, it will end. If I had a stock tip that guaranteed a return greater than any wealth for all of eternity, you would jump on it instantly. God guarantees us eternal rewards if we invest in eternity.

Another purpose is found in Romans 12:1-2, "I beseech you therefore, brethren, by the mercies of God, that ye present your bodies a living sacrifice, holy, acceptable unto God, which is your reasonable service. And be not conformed to this world: but be ye transformed by the renewing of your mind, that ye may prove what is that good, and acceptable, and perfect, will of God." So, how do you accomplish this purpose? The world wants to attack your faith and have you conform to their beliefs. It is important that you have a good foundation in faith, or the world will tear it apart. Your belief system has to be rock-solid.

What do you believe? I know many people who are adamant about their beliefs but don't know why they believe them. Some people focus on one area really strongly but are lax in other areas. For instance, a person might wear the most modest of dresses, but then watch rated "R" movies. Do you have opinions or do you have solid beliefs? Many people get their beliefs from other people. You might think just like your parents, or you might think just like your college professor, but have you really put some thoughts in your beliefs? Borrowed beliefs are dangerous. What if the person with whom you get your beliefs is wrong? There was a story of a young couple who had just gotten married. They were celebrating their first Thanksgiving together. The young wife was in the kitchen preparing the turkey when her new husband walked in and observed her doing something very strange. She was using a butcher knife to cut off about two inches off each end of the turkey. He asked her why she was doing that, and she told him it was the way her mom had prepared the turkey. He asked her again, "Why?" She stopped and thought for a moment and decided to call her mom. Her mom told her she observed the girl's grandmother doing it, so the young wife called her grandmother. Her grandmother told her that the reason she cut the ends off the turkey was because her oven was small and the turkey rarely ever fit. The pattern had been handed down to two generations before someone understood why. A belief that is borrowed is a dangerous belief because you might not know the reasons behind the belief. If you study and find what you believe, you will see how the foundation is built and you can tackle the tough issues and hold to them. Since we are all responsible for our beliefs, how can we be sure we have the right beliefs?

    You have to start out with the right foundation. The most important part of any structure is the foundation. In the building of your beliefs, a solid foundation will keep the rest of the structure from crumbling. If you have a weak foundation, your beliefs will be torn down. The world has changed its opinions on things constantly throughout history. Ken Davis in his book *How to Speak to Youth* told a story of his college speech class. He was given the assignment to creatively drive home a point in a memorable way. He chose the law of the pendulum which states that a pendulum can never return to a point higher than the point from which it was released. He attached a 3-foot string to a toy and suspended it from the top of the blackboard. He released it and marked how high it went every time it swung back. The marks on the chalk board got lower and lower. He asked the class if they believed the law of the pendulum. They all raised their hands including the teacher. Ken then asked the teacher to further assist him in the demonstration. The teacher complied and sat on a chair against the wall. Ken had rigged a 250 lb. weight to hang from four cords of 500 lb. test parachute cord (which supports eight times the needed weight). He brought the weight up to the nose of the teacher and held it there. He explained the law again and assured the teacher he had nothing to worry about. He asked the teacher if he still believed the law, and after a long pause and a few beads of sweat, the teacher nodded yes. Ken dropped the weight, and it swung across the room to the end of the arc and then began to swing back toward the teacher. Ken said he never saw someone move out of the way so fast. The teacher's foundation for believing the law was weak. He thought he knew what he believed, but it was a borrowed belief. He witnessed it in smaller scale, but he didn't believe it enough to risk his life. If you have a strong foundation for your beliefs, not even the threat of death won't move you.

  The strongest foundation is a perfect one, a foundation that is solid and without flaws, a foundation that has withstood the test of time and repeated attacks. The best foundation is one based on the Bible, but your approach to building on that foundation has to be correct. Some people use the Bible to prove their own beliefs instead of finding out what the Bible says and changing themselves to match the Bible. For example, some people believe that God won't send people to Hell, because He is a loving God. Their beliefs are based on feelings and their desires, but not on what the Bible says. Imagine if you were driving down the street in a sports car and you had a nice, smooth straightaway. The adrenaline kicks in, and you decide to floor it. You pass the speed limit at 45 MPH and keep going. You hit 65, then 85, then 105 and pretty soon you're 70 MPH over the speed limit. As you begin to slow, the rev of the engine dies down and you hear a high-pitched sound coming from behind you. You begin to glance up at your rearview mirror to investigate, and the mirror is filled with red and blue lights. Your heart sinks, but you have a plan. After pulling over, the officer approaches and asks you to step out of the car. He pulls his cuffs out and takes you to jail. You still have no worries because your belief is right. You're brought in to see the judge about your reckless driving, and the judge asks you the question in which you've been waiting: "Did you not see the speed limit sign?" You smile and eagerly answer, "I did, but I felt that the speed limit is more of a suggestion, and if we're really good drivers, it's okay to go as fast as we want." No matter what you feel, you're gonna stand before that judge, guilty. As absurd as this sounds, millions of people in the world have a feeling or belief that is just as absurd when compared to God's specific laws. These people decide what they want to believe and then go to the Bible and pick out little parts of passages and pull them out of context to prove what they believe. This is a shaky foundation that will cause their beliefs to fall, whether in this life or before the throne of God. This shaky foundation tries to tell a perfect God what is right and wrong. The best foundation is the Word of God. You can always fall back on the phrase, "It's what the Bible says." Once you set the Bible as your foundation, your structure will not fail.

  To make sure you study the perfect foundation correctly and know how to build on it, you need to consider a few rules. Rule 1–Read the whole passage. You can distort anything by pulling out bits and pieces and reconstructing the words. If you read the whole passage, you can get the thought behind it and understand the reasoning. Rule 2–Find out to whom the passage is written. Some passages are written to people who are saved, and some people have taken those passages to prove things that aren't true by applying them to the unsaved. Rule 3–Compare Scripture with Scripture. Don't compare scripture with a commentary. The commentator might be wrong. Take passages that talk about the same things and compare them and see what they say. The Bible will support itself. Rule 4–Have an open mind and heart and ask God to teach you. Sometimes, things that are good for you don't feel good. A doctor occasionally has to use a needle to help an infirmity or pull on a bone to set it after it breaks. We have tender areas in our lives that the Bible wants to fix, but sometimes it hurts. The final product is far better than the continued illness. If you have an open mind and let God teach you, you can be confident that your beliefs will be right, and then your life will have the right faith and purpose.

chapter 5

"The smallest speck is seen on snow."
–John Gay

In 1992, my sister went on a ladies' retreat with her church and left her husband, Jamey, unattended. I was twelve years old at the time and was in his care. Unbeknownst to his wife, he packed up the kids and headed down to the car dealership. It was my first time at a car dealership. My two nephews and I hung out in a small waiting room for what seemed to be hours, while Jamey haggled with the salesman over a price. I was amazed at his patience. Pontiac had just come out with their new look, and the Grand Am was their flagship. It was a sleek, new look that no other car manufacturer had accomplished with flare during that time. Jamey got the price and options he wanted, and soon after, we were getting into his new vehicle. It was clean. It was pretty. It had a new car smell. No one had driven it before. It was only his car. He had the confidence that no one had ever crashed the car, smoked in the car, or did who knows what to it. I was so excited for him. I sat in a brand-new car for the first time. I'll never forget the experience. There was something nice about being in a new car. It was different than buying a used car. His new car was treated with the best of respect.

In 2007, I had a similar experience. My truck was breaking down, and I needed a new one. My wife and I researched trucks in our area and found that the best deal on the GMC Canyon that I wanted was at a Ford dealership. We drove down and test drove the vehicle. It ran great. It had 30,000 miles on it. We bought it, but noticed some things in it later. The rearview mirror was not the original. In fact, it didn't even go with the truck. The windshield had been replaced. There was a smoke smell inside which we spent hours trying to get out. There were cigarette burns I didn't previously notice. One of the plastic pieces had broken on it. And, it had its basic wear and tear that comes with 30,000 miles of truck driving. I began to wonder what the previous owner had done with the truck. Why did it have its windshield replaced? I still think about its past, and I'm not comfortable with it.

Now equate these vehicles to people. The first was a pure vehicle. It had only had one driver–Jamey. The second was used, had some defects, and wasn't as nice. A life that has a disregard for purity is far worse than a second-hand vehicle. Society loves to make "used cars" out of people. The pressure is all around you. Companies sell to your sexual desires because it is a powerful inroad to your thought process and memory. People around you will pressure you into doing something impure because it makes you like one of them, and that makes them feel better.

In every medium imaginable, society has diluted the minds of men with impurity. In one minute of TV, you can be bombarded by multiple ads for lingerie, toiletry such as shavers and soap that show nudity, vacation spots that have women in bikinis, and even hamburger joints that use a model to sell their burgers. It used to be that TV was wholesome and wouldn't dare reveal anything close to what they do now. But TV is just the tip of the iceberg. The monster is the internet. According to statistics from toptenreviews.com, there are 4.2 million pornographic websites with 72 million visitors a month to pornographic sites worldwide. Eighty percent of teens from the ages of 15-17 have had pornographic exposures. Every

39 minutes, a new pornographic video is being produced (www.toptenreviews.com).

Let's say that you go to church three times a week for a total of 7 hours. You do your devotions 20 minutes a day, seven days-a-week. You're up to a little over 9 hours of exposure to God and His word. According to A. C. Nielson Co., the average American watches 4 hours of TV a day. That's 28 hours a week that you're being bombarded with impurity. On the battlefront of a man's mind, the devil is unleashing three times the volleys than the church is. This only accounts for TV. It doesn't include magazine ads, billboards, newspapers, etc.

So, how do we battle back? Man rarely starts impurity with the physical. His first battle is the mind. The body will act on the mind's thoughts. A pattern is given in the Bible that shows the tragedy of a loose mind and its affects on a man. II Samuel 13 records the story:

1 And it came to pass after this, that Absalom the son of David had a fair sister, whose name was Tamar; and Amnon the son of David loved her.
2 And Amnon was so vexed, that he fell sick for his sister Tamar; for she was a virgin; and Amnon thought it hard for him to do any thing to her.
3 But Amnon had a friend, whose name was Jonadab, the son of Shimeah David's brother: and Jonadab was a very subtil man.
4 And he said unto him, Why art thou, being the king's son, lean from day to day? wilt thou not tell me? And Amnon said unto him, I love Tamar, my brother Absalom's sister.
5 And Jonadab said unto him, Lay thee down on thy bed, and make thyself sick: and when thy father cometh to see thee, say unto him, I pray thee, let my sister Tamar come, and give me meat, and dress the meat in my sight, that I may see it, and eat it at her hand.
6 So Amnon lay down, and made himself sick: and when the king was come to see him, Amnon said unto the king, I pray thee, let Tamar my sister come, and make me a couple of cakes in my sight, that I may eat at her hand.
7 Then David sent home to Tamar, saying, Go now to thy brother Amnon's house, and dress him meat.
8 So Tamar went to her brother Amnon's house; and he was laid down. And she took flour, and kneaded it, and made cakes in his sight, and did bake the cakes.
9 And she took a pan, and poured them out before him; but he refused to eat. And Amnon said, Have out all men from me. And they went out every man from him.
10 And Amnon said unto Tamar, Bring the meat into the chamber, that I may

eat of thine hand. And Tamar took the cakes which she had made, and brought them into the chamber to Amnon her brother.
11 And when she had brought them unto him to eat, he took hold of her, and said unto her, Come lie with me, my sister.
12 And she answered him, Nay, my brother, do not force me; for no such thing ought to be done in Israel: do not thou this folly.
13 And I, whither shall I cause my shame to go? and as for thee, thou shalt be as one of the fools in Israel. Now therefore, I pray thee, speak unto the king; for he will not withhold me from thee.
14 Howbeit he would not hearken unto her voice: but, being stronger than she, forced her, and lay with her.
15 Then Amnon hated her exceedingly; so that the hatred wherewith he hated her was greater than the love wherewith he had loved her. And Amnon said unto her, Arise, be gone.
16 And she said unto him, There is no cause: this evil in sending me away is greater than the other that thou didst unto me. But he would not hearken unto her.

The first step in the pattern toward impurity is wrong thoughts. Your thoughts make-up who you are. They are the front lines of the battle. Amnon put a lot of thought into his desires for Tamar, so much so that he was vexed and became sick. Once the Devil gets a foothold, he'll never let you forget it and will attempt to takeover your life. A story was once told of a young couple who lived a few hundred years ago and owned a small house that overlooked the ocean. They fed themselves with a garden and enjoyed the beautiful view. One day, a strange man knocked on their door and offered them a large amount of money for the house. After much debate, they decided to sell the house and buy a large house in a distant land. After moving, they realized the size of the house didn't make that much of a difference and they missed their old house. Soon after, they were back to that small house begging the strange man to sell it back to them. He refused, but they continued to beg. He thought for a minute and told them it would cost more than the price that they sold it to him, and the couple agreed. He then told them he gets to keep one thing–a spike nailed in the doorpost. It seemed odd to them, but they quickly agreed and soon were moved back to their little house overlooking the ocean. It was wonderful. But one day a putrid smell met their noses. They began to feel nauseated and began to investigate. After much searching, they opened the front door and discovered an animal carcass hanging from the spike on the doorpost. The couple began to remove it, but a voice in the distance cried for them to stop. Upon looking up, they saw the strange man running their way. He yelled, "Don't touch my property!" The argument ensued and the local constable was called. After hearing both sides, the strange man won. The couple stormed inside and vowed they could handle the smell and were not going to leave the house. Months past, and no matter what they did, they couldn't handle it. It wasn't long after that that the house became vacant and the strange man moved back in. The couple couldn't bear the smell.

    You see, the male mind is a steel trap. Once the devil gets one thought of impurity staked into the doorpost of your mind, it will be there for decades to come. The stench from the putrid image stored there will corrupt the rest of you. That memory can lie dormant for years and resurface at some random time. Your impure memories will betray you. They will corrupt your thought processes, but there is one difference between your mind and the story told–you can't move out of your mind.

    If you give in to your sexual desires and allow your mind to wander, it will get calloused to the Holy Spirit's conviction. Your thoughts will continually rehearse the images stored in your mind, and you will begin to apply them to women around you. Soon, your thoughts will be impure about women you see, just as Amnon's thoughts were about his sister. The thought process on impurity is easier to attack at the beginning stages than it is in the advanced stages. You can liken impure thoughts to a drug. It's addicting and always leaves you wanting more. Your mind will focus on something small, but the next time you allow your impure thoughts to run wild, they will need something greater to fulfill the desire, then something greater, then greater, then greater, until the impure thoughts consume you. Not only will impurity corrupt your mind, it will corrupt your communication.

    Your mouth speaks what's in your mind. Amnon not only thought about Tamar in a worng way, he told his friend his evil desires. Now, because of Amnon's corrupted communication, another man is involved in his sin. As stated before, man is in a battle against society for the purity of his mind. Satan doesn't need the help of a man's friends, but he will capitalize on it if offered. In speaking about his desires, Amnon gave the devil an open door with which to attack him. His communication was helping to bring down his friends. If it weren't for Amnon's loose mouth, Jonadab may have never known of Amnon's desires, and would not have given the advice he did. Jonadab formed a plan, communicated it to Amnon, and the plan followed the next step in impurity–the step of action.

"Be not deceived: evil communications corrupt good manners" (I Cor. 15:33). The evil communication leads to the impure action. As in Amnon's case, the action was horrendous. He raped his own sister. Many impure actions are horrible in nature–a woman is raped; a girl loses her purity, gets pregnant, or a disease is passed on; a child is molested; the list goes on. You might think, "I would never do something that severe." I Cor. 10:12 says, "Wherefore let him that thinketh he standeth take heed lest he fall." Remember that when you pick a path, you also pick the destination of the path. As you travel down the path, it might start off seeming innocent, but as time goes on, you get calloused to things along the path. Things that you used to think were horrible are now not that bad. When you reach the end of the path and finish performing an impure action, you're emotions and hormones will no longer be as strong, and your mind will be clear to realize the guilt or the consequence of what you just did. Amnon, when he had fulfilled his lust, realized what he did and hated Tamar because of his sin. She was all he could think about one moment, then his actions led him to hate her. The actions did not bring the happiness he imagined. Not only did he disgrace himself and her, his actions lead to her brother killing him. Ask the rapist where the pattern started. Ask the pedophile where the pattern started. Ask the HIV patient where it all started. The consequences of the path of impurity are a result of a pattern of impure thoughts. It's a horrible thing to find yourself at the end of that path.

So how do you combat the flesh and Satan? Remember how it was mentioned earlier that you can't move out of your mind? That phrase is true and harsh and seems detrimental, but God offers a solution which is found in Ephesians 4:22-24, "That ye put off concerning the former conversation the old man, which is corrupt according to the deceitful lusts; And be renewed in the spirit of your mind; And that ye put on the new man, which after God is created in righteousness and true holiness." God says that you are to put off that former conversation, or lifestyle, and to renew your mind. You can't move out of your mind, but you can renew it and ask God to help you focus on pure things. You can have daily devotions to help you focus on the things of God.

The next step is found three verses later, "Neither give place to the devil." Just like that strange man that wanted that couple's house, the devil wants a small place in your life, so he can take over. Every time an impure thought begins to enter your brain, attack it by thinking on God's Holy Word. Recite a verse such as, "I will set no wicked thing before mine eyes: I hate the work of them that turn aside; it shall not cleave to me" (Psalm 101:3). Other passages that can help are II Corinthians 10:3-5, I Corinthians 9:27, and Romans 12:1-2.

The last step is to cut the amount of times the devil can tempt you. The earlier statistic stated that the devil is sending out three times the influence the church is. You can cut the devil's number down greatly. Stay away from the temptation. If you don't want impure images shown to you, don't watch TV. Don't go on the internet, or have it so a family member (preferably of the opposite sex) is around you the whole time. Have a woman go through a magazine before you look at it, and have her edit out all the bad images. Don't read books that have impure communication. Don't be alone with a member of the opposite sex if you are not married to them. If you can't handle the heat (and we can't), don't go in the kitchen.

If you follow these steps, you'll be able to live a pure life which will bring you many benefits. We talked about the difference between the new car and the used car and how it's related to people. Which one do you want? Which one do you want to be? My wife took a vow of purity when she was in highschool, which was a public school in Ohio. When her ten-year class reunion came, we traveled there to attend. We sat at a table where a lot of her friends were, and they all had one question–"Was it worth it?" They wouldn't know. They had all lost their purity before marriage. Ten years had passed, and her classmates still hadn't grown up. My wife didn't have to answer the question. During the conversation, I was oblivious to what they were talking about. I found out later what the conversation was about and I answered the question for her with joyful tears in my eyes–YES!!! The greatest gift my wife has ever given me or will ever give me is her devoted purity for the man she married–me. Far greater than knowing there's no history to a new car I own is knowing that there's no history to my wife. There's not a man that I will one day meet that has seen her naked or performed impure acts with her. I don't have to worry about where she's been or what past relationships she's had because there are none, and she has saved herself for me. I was also honored to give her the gift of my purity.

Another benefit is found in II Timothy 2:20-21, "But in a great house there are not only vessels of gold and of silver, but also of wood and of earth; and some to honour and some to dishonour. If a man therefore purge himself from these, he shall be a vessel unto honour, sanctified, and meet for the master's use, and prepared unto every good work." What kind of vessel do you want to give God? When I go to get a cup in which to pour my favorite drink, I don't start looking in the work room where all my tools are. If I were to do that, I would find a cup that may have dust on it, or a spider web inside, or maybe some paint inside, or even some grease. I want a cup that is sparkling clean. I don't want dust from floating skin particles or random chemicals in my drink. I don't want foreign substances that might be harmful to me or change the taste of my favorite drink. And I definitely don't want a spider and/or spider web in my drink. I want a vessel that is fit for my use. Why would God, then, want a vessel that is full of impure thoughts and actions that will hinder His testimony and corrupt the message? God can and will do great things through us if we are pure and sanctified for His use.

Another benefit is that of being an example. You may think that impurity isn't that important now, but will you think the same way when you have gone down the path, reaped the consequences, learned your lesson, and now have kids of your own that are fighting temptation. Your kids one day will look to you as an example and will base their decisions on the ones you have made. They may even use you as an excuse. Your daughter some day will be interested in boys. Do you want her to find a boy just like you were? She will subconsciously look for someone like you. What about a son? Do you want him to fail in the same struggles you once did, or do you want him to succeed? The choice is yours. It would be a great thing to tell your children one day that you were able to accomplish purity, and that they can too.

Purity is every man's struggle. Satan knows the inroads to a man and will fight dirty, but by taking the right steps, a man can be a vessel fit for the master's use, and will then be able to reap all the benefits of a pure life. Are you up for the challenge?

chapter 6

*"Management is doing things right;
leadership is doing the right things."*
–Peter F. Drucker

Were you ever asked to be in charge of something where you really didn't want to be in charge? In high school, I was nominated to run for school president. It sounded fun and regal, until I got the position. It was a lot of work with no thanks! A few months later, the principal asked me to be the senior coordinator, the one in charge of fund-raising and the senior trip. I learned my lesson with the last position and was a little leery. After a lot of work, it turned out well, and I was happy with what the class accomplished. I was now ready for college. I could just sit back and coast and stay in the shadows. Nope. The staff wanted me to be in charge of a soulwinning group. What a scary thing for me! There was so much responsibility and work. A few years later, they decided I was the best person to become a bus captain in the worst part of a neighboring city. I told the staff, "no." They persisted and won. I had no clue how to run a bus route, but the bus workers were patient and followed my leading and worked hard, and we were one of the top three routes for three years. One of my professors pointed me to John C. Maxwell's leadership books which helped me tremendously. I was excited when I got hired to work at First Baptist Church of Bridgeport, Ml. I thought, "Wow, I can finally rest and take a break from the bus." When I attended my first Sunday, Pastor Ouellette introduced me to an assistant pastor and asked him to show me the video room where I would be working. I stood in the video room during the service and noticed some things that weren't convenient, and I offered some solutions. The guy running the projector turned around and said, "Whatever you want. You're in charge." My heart was suddenly in my throat and my jaw probably hit the floor. I couldn't even muster a "What???!!!" I knew how to make graphics, but nothing how to present them on projectors, web, print, video, etc. It was overwhelming to hear that statement. Pretty soon I was running the projector, teaching a Sunday school class, and teaching a bus class. No matter where I go, I get thrown into leadership roles. I've learned a lot over the years and in reading books, but I'm not an expert, and I still dread the positions.

  J. Oswald Sanders said, "Leadership is influence, the ability of one person to influence others to follow his or her lead." When placed in this position, there is an implied command to influence. The position given to someone does not guarantee that the people under that position will follow. An old Chinese proverb says, "He who thinketh he leadeth and hath no followers is only going for a walk." You can be put into a position, but if you don't know how to lead, you're just going for a walk with no one following. Neither does this mean that you have to be placed in a leadership position to influence people. I heard a statistic one time that said the most introverted person (shy person) influences 10,000 people in his lifetime. Your actions might be noticed by someone who then chooses to follow your pattern. No matter what, you're going to be faced with some type of leadership position in your life. As a man, you're required to lead your family. Do you know how to properly lead? Do you know how to keep followers that are happy to serve under you?

  There have been numerous horrible leaders throughout history.

These men have amassed a great following but have not led well. They have instilled false beliefs in their followers and will one day be held accountable for their actions. Genghis Kahn led his men in killing whole villages of friendly communities so that he may gain power. Nero wrapped Christians in flammable material and burned them in his garden like candles to provide light at night. He also set Rome on fire and blamed the Christians. Hitler convinced the Germans that the Aryan race was supreme and all others should be subject to them. Saddam killed his own citizens to keep control over Iraq. These are some of the great leaders of history whose names are remembered because they had an ability to lead but did not do right things with it. If you have the ability to influence, you too will be held accountable someday for how you lead.

If there were only two people on earth, both of them would be leaders. Psalm 27:17 says, "Iron sharpeneth iron; so a man sharpeneth the countenance of his friend." They will both influence each other. You might think your lot in life is insignificant, but it's not. Did you ever see the movie, "It's a Wonderful Life," not the colored version, the black and white one (it's better). As cliché as it is, it paints a good picture that one life, no matter how insignificant it is, can influence a great deal. What did you think when you read that I thought the black and white version was better? You formed an agreement with my idea which reinforced a positive paradigm about me, or you formed a disagreement which reinforced a negative tendency toward my beliefs. Either way, I influenced you. One small opinion on your behalf will influence another. Since leadership is influence, you have no choice in the matter. You are a leader. Maybe you think that leadership isn't that important to God. Well, if you count how many times "leader" is used in the Bible, you come up with three. There you go. With that statistic, you might think leadership isn't important to God. Well, think about this. The word "servant" is found in the Bible 462 times. That's a big difference. Moses, one of the greatest leaders of all time (especially in the Bible), was referred to by God as "Moses, my servant." God refers to Himself (Christ) as a servant. Isaiah 42:1 says, "Behold my servant, whom

I uphold; mine elect, in whom my soul delighteth; I have put my spirit on him: he shall bring forth judgment to the Gentiles." Christ is the greatest leader of all times. His life turned the world upside down. I would consider that influence. Yet, God doesn't call Him a leader. He calls Him a servant. If you've ever held a leadership position, you'll find that leadership is mainly comprised of service. Service is the key to it. You cannot lead effectively without serving. Many men take the wrong path to leadership and don't perform the position correctly.

These men may push their way to leadership. Lucifer tried to push his way into a greater role than he held. In doing so, a third of the angels followed him and now share his fate. A leader might try to step into a leadership role because he wants to control people. Number 16:1-5 tells of one such man:

> *1 Now Korah, the son of Izhar, the son of Kohath, the son of Levi, and Dathan and Abiram, the sons of Eliab, and On, the son of Peleth, sons of Reuben, took men:*
> *2 And they rose up before Moses, with certain of the children of Israel, two hundred and fifty princes of the assembly, famous in the congregation, men of renown:*
> *3 And they gathered themselves together against Moses and against Aaron, and said unto them, Ye take too much upon you, seeing all the congregation are holy, every one of them, and the LORD is among them: wherefore then lift ye up yourselves above the congregation of the LORD?*
> *4 And when Moses heard it, he fell upon his face:*
> *5 And he spake unto Korah and unto all his company, saying, Even to morrow the LORD will shew who are his, and who is holy; and will cause him to come near unto him: even him whom he hath chosen will he cause to come near unto him.*

Korah overstepped his boundaries and tried to take authority when he was not given it. Some men of Israel gave him authority, but God didn't. God chose to abase Korah later in the chapter:

> *31 And it came to pass, as he had made an end of speaking all these words, that the ground clave asunder that was under them:*
> *32 And the earth opened her mouth, and swallowed them up, and their houses, and all the men that appertained unto Korah, and all their goods.*

33 They, and all that appertained to them, went down alive into the pit, and the earth closed upon them: and they perished from among the congregation.
34 And all Israel that were round about them fled at the cry of them: for they said, Lest the earth swallow us up also.
35 And there came out a fire from the LORD, and consumed the two hundred and fifty men that offered incense.

Korah went up against the man of God, and God punished him. It is not our place to seek control.

Another wrong path to leadership is the one that seeks fame. It is a quest to fulfill one's pride. Mark 10:35-41 tells of such a story.

35 And James and John, the sons of Zebedee, come unto him, saying, Master, we would that thou shouldest do for us whatsoever we shall desire.
36 And he said unto them, What would ye that I should do for you?
37 They said unto him, Grant unto us that we may sit, one on thy right hand, and the other on thy left hand, in thy glory.
38 But Jesus said unto them, Ye know not what ye ask: can ye drink of the cup that I drink of? and be baptized with the baptism that I am baptized with?
39 And they said unto him, We can. And Jesus said unto them, Ye shall indeed drink of the cup that I drink of; and with the baptism that I am baptized withal shall ye be baptized:
40 But to sit on my right hand and on my left hand is not mine to give; but it shall be given to them for whom it is prepared.
41 And when the ten heard it, they began to be much displeased with James and John.

To desire prominence where it is not offered is not wise. Christ warned James and John that the road there was not a pleasant one, but they persisted. He told them they would still have to travel that rough path, but He couldn't give them the position they desired.

Christ, in a few verses later, gives the right path to leadership: "But so shall it not be among you: but whosoever will be great among you, shall be your minister: And whosoever of you will be the chiefest, shall be servant of all" (Mark 10:43-44). He said that to be great, you must serve. It goes against many popular beliefs of man. Some will say seniority merits promotion. Some may say education or knowledge will merit a promotion. Man may think that, but God says promotion comes to those who first serve. "For promotion cometh neither from the east, nor from the west, nor from the south. But God is the judge: he putteth down one, and setteth up another" (Psalm 75:6-7). God promotes those whom He chooses. Joseph, for example, spent years as a slave and a prisoner before attaining a high position. In that time, he served and invested in others, and God rewarded him.

God has given us a path to attain a leadership position, but when you get the position, will you be commended or condemned for the way you lead? As mentioned before, you will influence, and you will have to account for how you influence. "For unto whomsoever much is given, of him shall be much required" (Luke 12:48b). If God leads you to a leadership position, such as the head of a family or a group, you'll want to keep in mind a few requirements.

First off, you have to have a willingness to serve others and put their needs before your own (Mark 10:43-44). I've found that the way I treat my wife determines the response I get. Ephesians 5:28 tells men to love their wives as a man loves his own body. As I give up my desires, and prefer my wife above myself, it brings out a willingness in her to follow my direction. For example, if I help clean the house, or do dishes, or go where she wants to go out to eat, I have no problem giving direction. She feels loved and is willing to submit. By both of us preferring the other greater than ourselves, we both get returns on our investments. But, I have to be willing to put her needs before mine and take the first step.

Another attribute you need is a desire to seek God primarily. Paul says in Philippians 3:10 that he would give up all to know Christ. Then, seven verses later, he tells us to follow his lead as he seeks to know Christ (also I Cor. 11:1). If my pastor's heart and goals don't match mine, and I lead people in the wrong direction, I'll be held accountable for the mess I make and the counter-production caused. For all Christians to move forward, we must all be like-minded. That means the leaders must have the same desire–to know God's heart.

In addition to knowing God's heart, a leader needs to depend on

God and not himself. "I am the vine, ye are the branches: He that abideth in me, and I in him, the same bringeth forth much fruit: for without me ye can do nothing" (John 15:5). Branches are not able to draw nutrients out of the ground. They are not able to hold themselves up in a storm. Branches cannot exist without the vine. The vine provides spiritual nourishment and support in tough times as well as the good. If a branch tries to exist without the vine, it will wither and die or fall when the storm comes. A good leader has to have support from God.

He also needs to seek humility instead of fame. The same man who said to follow him as he follows Christ also said, "For I know that in me (that is, in my flesh,) dwelleth no good thing" (Rom. 7:18). Man has sought fame for thousands of years, only to find it is not what it is cracked-up to be. Princess Diana died in an auto accident in an attempt to escape the paparazzi. Fame killed her. Actors of late have committed suicide because of their empty lives they thought would be fulfilled by fame. Humility will reap greater rewards in leadership than will a prideful desire for fame.

A leader must also be a man of vision. "Where there is no vision, the people perish: but he that keepeth the law, happy is he" (Pro. 29:18). Have you ever been to a party that was dead? For my wife's ten-year class reunion, we traveled to Ohio to attend it. Much of the class showed up, but the class president didn't do much to prepare for the occasion. After eating the dinner, one event had technical difficulties and there were no other events planned. The class began to grumble and leave their separate ways. It was a bad party because the leadership didn't have a vision. The people who follow you want to stay active and move forward, so you must have a vision for the future.

With all the requirements, there are also many costs to accompany a leadership role. The leader will face self-sacrifice numerous times. When a follower fails to perform a task, it often falls on the leader. He will also face social loneliness because there are some burdens that can't be shared to others. Fatigue also becomes a factor. Often a leader will face criticism. Everyone has an opinion on the way things should be done, and they rarely keep their criticisms to themselves. People will also reject the leader and/or the decisions he makes. Then, on top of that, the leader has great pressure. He is responsible for his actions and where he leads others.

The costs of leading are not without reward though. As mentioned in Mark, if we lead by serving, we are number one in God's eyes. God exalts those that humble themselves. In addition to God exalting you when you lead God's way, those who follow you will succeed also, and the eternal rewards will far outlast earthly fame and earthly pleasures.

financial stability
the road less traveled

chapter 7

"They who are of the opinion that Money will do everything, may very well be suspected to do everything for Money."
–George Savile,

    While teaching a teen guys Sunday school class, I did an experiment. I took a Hollister Co. advertisement, cut off the title, and photoshopped a geeky guy's face over the original model's face. I presented the picture to the guys I taught and asked what they thought of the guy in the picture. Immediately, they all said he was a nerd. I asked what they thought of his clothes, and they were indifferent. I then showed them the real picture with the Hollister title and the model's face. They all wanted to change their opinions about the clothes. Their thought processes didn't make any sense at all. Why were these teen guys so enamored with the moniker "Hollister"? Did they think that they would be accepted if they wore the clothes? I had just proved to them that the clothes don't matter, yet they had been indoctrinated by their friends, by companies trying to make a profit, and by society in general. As a teen, they can long for the $40 shirt, but rarely have the means (in themselves) to purchase it. That natural financial restraint might last through the teen years, but as soon as the teen gets a job, he often times buy things he's always wanted or thinks he needs not realizing the error of his investment.

The trap of society calls for its captor to buy the newest items, for in doing so, the captor will be accepted and have true happiness. Do you remember when you were a child, and the new toy came out? There were so many when I was a kid. We had G.I. Joes, Transformers, Legos, video games, and so much more. Now when you think about all those toys you played with, do you still play with them on a daily basis? No. You moved on to different things. Yet, as a child, you stood in the aisle of the store staring at the toy, thinking, "If I could only have that toy . . ." Where is it now? The toy didn't bring you everlasting joy. We buy something and are excited for a short time, then the novelty wears off, and we fall for the next advertisement telling us we need something else to make us happy. Trust me. I know the evil plots of the companies and my flesh, and I still fall in the trap.

Companies are in business to make money, and they're good at it. They want your money and will do anything to get it. They will lie and show the greatest ad to you, so you'll walk in their store and help support their upper-level management's glamorous lifestyle. They advertise to everyone and convince others they need the items, so now you have your friends and neighbors advertising to you, too. It can be equated to the common story of the zombies. You start with one zombie that bites a person, and that person then becomes a zombie. Now you have two zombies that go out and bite people. Pretty soon you have four, then eight, and so on. The process never ends. With so many items offered by so many companies, too bad these zombies don't have enough money to buy everything. But wait! There's always credit cards! They can buy now and pay later. Oops! Another person just got bit because credit cards are companies that want your money, too. They aren't a friend who will loan you money without charging you. They want to make as much money as they can off the money they loan out. After getting into $20,000 in debt (it's not hard) and a bunch of empty possessions, the zombie can't afford the credit card payments. With such a draw on his bank account, he cannot afford the things which produce money such as a college degree or investments. He can't buy a car because his credit is trash, and he can't afford to fix the old car he has because of his credit card bills. I mentioned $20,000 earlier, and that might be a little extreme, so let's drop it to $7,000. At $7,000, $200 is required each month to pay back the credit card company. But, only $150 is actually going to the amount he owes. Fifty of it goes to the credit card company to pay interest and finance charges. That makes 47 payments (4 years) of $200 and the credit card company made $2,350 of profit off of him. And that's based on a moderately good interest rate of 8%. I said all that just to say, "Retail and credit card companies are not his friends, neither are they yours."

I used to believe I could have a credit card and be disciplined. I told myself I would only use it for emergencies. It was amazing what things became "emergencies." I spent more than I earned a month because I had some faulty core beliefs. I'll list some of these faulty core beliefs, and while you read them, ask yourself (and answer yourself honestly) if you have any of these.

1. "I deserve _____ (fill in the blank)." Did you know that because person "A" has something, doesn't mean person "B" deserves the same thing. When I was a bus captain, I purchased a large bag of candy weekly. On occasion, I would give a child candy because I noticed something that they had done that was worth reward. After rewarding them, the kid in the next seat told me it wasn't fair and told me I was a jerk. How was it not fair? I worked and made money to buy the candy. It's my candy. I can do what I want with it. I could give it all to one kid if I wanted. Because others have things we don't, doesn't mean we deserve to have them, too. "For promotion cometh neither from the east, nor from the west, nor from the south. But God is the judge: he putteth down one, and setteth up another" (Ps. 75:6-7).

2. "I have to have _____ to be accepted or happy." We've already discussed how this philosophy doesn't work.

3. "Buying now and paying later is a good choice." As mentioned before, credit cards are not your friends. You almost always pay more later than you do at the beginning.

4. "Expensive entertainment is fulfilling." If this were true, you could watch one football game (pick your sport) or one TV show and be set for the rest of your life. You might argue that entertainment is fulfilling when you do it on a regular basis. You'll find that it's not so much the activity that is fulfilling, but being able to share the experience with others. Ever go to a sporting event, theme park, etc. by yourself? If you have, was it that great? The sharing of an event with another person is what brings enjoyment in most cases. On top of that, expensive entertainment is... expensive. I went to a Michigan game this year and spent $116 a ticket, and that was just for a college game! It wasn't even a professional game. On top of that, I stood in the freezing rain and snow for three hours. I did it one time for the experience with a friend of mine that was visiting from out of state. As much as I like Michigan and football, I'm probably not ever going to buy another ticket.

Until you ask yourself the reasoning for the purchase of an item and whether you can afford it in the long run, you will not be financially stable. I'm not saying that you can't ever buy anything you want. I'm saying, buying things you want shouldn't consume you or rule your life. You don't want to dig yourself into a ditch in which you can't get out.

So, how do you choose the best investments for life? Which ones will actually bring the most joy and return? Let's take each one into account. Now, before, I had mentioned that companies aren't your friends, and creditors aren't either, but there are possibilities to use credit to your advantage. For instance, there are credit card companies that put bait on a hook so they can reel people in. If a person is *truly* disciplined, they can take the bait and not get hooked. One of my friends is this type of person. He has a credit card that gives him airline miles with every purchase. He uses the card only for gas and food and then sends the check right away to cover it. When I asked him, he had enough miles to cover his flight to my wedding. Only the truly disciplined can play this game.

Credit cards also help build credit which will help you finance a house or car and get you a better rate. But, there are some things to keep in mind. Remember that they are in business to make money off of you. You can't trust their wonderful offers. Read the fine print. Some cards change rates after a period of time or after a failure to pay on time. Also, any balance that's not paid off right away will accrue charges and interest. That's money you could use to buy other things. Unless you're disciplined, credit is not a wise investment.

Other types of investing can include putting your money into a savings account, stocks, or mutual funds. As a child I was told to put my money in savings. I was taught to pinch every penny. My savings account gave me a 2% return. Later, I found that inflation (rise in price of items) was 3% a year. I was losing 1% a year! Below is a passage about saving your money:

Mt 25:14-28
14 For the kingdom of heaven is as a man travelling into a far country, who called his own servants, and delivered unto them his goods.
15 And unto one he gave five talents, to another two, and to another one; to every man according to his several ability; and straightway took his journey.
16 Then he that had received the five talents went and traded with the same, and made them other five talents.
17 And likewise he that had received two, he also gained other two.
18 But he that had received one went and digged in the earth, and hid his lord's money.
19 After a long time the lord of those servants cometh, and reckoneth with them.
20 And so he that had received five talents came and brought other five talents, saying, Lord, thou deliveredst unto me five talents: behold, I have gained beside them five talents more.
21 His lord said unto him, Well done, thou good and faithful servant: thou hast *been faithful over a few things, I will make thee ruler over many things: enter thou into the joy of thy lord.*
22 *He also that had received two talents came and said, Lord, thou deliveredst unto me two talents: behold, I have gained two other talents beside them.*
23 *His lord said unto him, Well done, good and faithful servant; thou hast been faithful over a few things, I will make thee ruler over many things: enter thou into the joy of thy lord.*

> 24 Then he which had received the one talent came and said, Lord, I knew thee that thou art an hard man, reaping where thou hast not sown, and gathering where thou hast not strawed:
> 25 And I was afraid, and went and hid thy talent in the earth: lo, there thou hast that is thine.
> 26 His lord answered and said unto him, Thou wicked and slothful servant, thou knewest that I reap where I sowed not, and gather where I have not strawed:
> 27 Thou oughtest therefore to have put my money to the exchangers, and then at my coming I should have received mine own with usury.
> 28 Take therefore the talent from him, and give it unto him which hath ten talents.

Hoarding your money doesn't get a return, and it doesn't help others, either.

Stocks help companies grow and they give you a return on your money, but they are very risky. The chances you'll hit a big return in a short time are extremely rare. Mutual funds are generally safer than stocks since you can have your money divided in different types of funds (diversification), so if one fund drops, usually the others stay good.

These all are ways of investing, with some good and some bad, but these investments all have one major flaw–they don't go with you when you die. While I was working nights, my wife was left home by herself in a neighborhood that wasn't too safe. After installing motion detector lights and training her how to use the handgun, I still didn't feel at ease. We began to pray for a dog that would help protect her and give her some company at night. Our friends had just bought an English Mastiff puppy and shortly after found out they were expecting a child. The soon-to-be mother realized she couldn't handle the smells of the puppy. They asked if we wanted the puppy, and we quickly accepted, not knowing how big of a dog this little puppy was going to be. The months of growth went by quickly, and her bark and growl deepened, making her a very large, intimidating dog. But, as she grew, we noticed that our dog favored me over my wife. She would obey me quicker, respond to my calls better, and would choose to lay on my side of the bed. The dog still loved and protected my wife, but no matter what my wife did, the dog still favored me.

It was not a matter of how good we were to her; it was a choice the dog made. You see, "No man [and no dog] can serve two masters: for either he will hate the one, and love the other; or else he will hold to the one, and despise the other. (Matt. 6:24a)" The dog cannot love us both equally. She has a favorite. In the same regards, you have a choice to make: who will you serve? The rest of Matthew 6:24 says, "Ye cannot serve God and mammon." Mammon is wealth as a focus of worship. Will you be a slave to money or a servant of God? You can't chase both. Chasing money and possessions leads you down a dead-end road, but investing in the things of God and trusting God has many benefits.

When you rely on God, it builds your faith and God makes Himself real to you. After a year of working as a clerk at a golf course during my college years, I became the manager. It was a great job that allowed me to "test the greens" (play a round of golf) and get payed for it. I was also able to hire other college students and give them a means to pay their college bills. After working two years as a manager, the general manager of the corporation visited the golf course and asked me to do some things that were unethical and illegal. I prayed all weekend about what to do, and God told me to quit my job. I still owed $550 on my college bill for the year, and I had no money. I called up the general manager and gave him my notice. He told me to wait, and he drove up the next day to convince me otherwise. I knew what God wanted me to do, and I stood firm. He understood and handed me my final check. It had a week's pay on it, a week's paid vacation which he didn't have to give me, and he also gave me a $50 bonus for doing a good job (he never gave bonuses). It came out to $550, the amount I owed. One problem–I didn't have any money on which to live. I began to pray again. That week, a sweet lady that took lessons at the golf course gave me a good-bye card and walked out. I opened it, and there was $120 inside! Praise the Lord! I had learned to rely on God. He became real to me. He wasn't just a head-knowledge. He proved himself to me. Investing in God builds your faith.

I've also found that God has a bigger shovel than I do. I can shovel money into "God's investment firm" and He fills the hole I just made, but His shovel is bigger. Just recently my wife and I attended our giving banquet at the church, and God told us to give $5,000 over the next year. I had no clue how we were going to do it. It didn't work out on paper, but we trusted God. God gave me overtime at my job, and we were making our payments with no problem. My wife's employer gave us 430 law books a few months later, which we were able to sell for $1,300. Then he gave us an unexpected check and we soon had $2,500 in our savings account (this is money extra to the monthly payments we were still giving to the church). I had some bad debt (from my immature years) of $7,500 that I owed a credit card company. I had been paying about $250 a month on it for five years ($15,000 total), and the balance barely budged due to a high interest rate, penalties, and finance charges. I called to see if by chance they would settle for $2,500, and they said "yes"! They threw away $5,000 of debt! We paid off the $5,000 commitment to the giving banquet that year and a $7,500 debt. God turned our $5,000 we gave to the church into a $12,500 value. If we were to have not made the commitment, none of it would have ever happened. God has a bigger shovel.

Investing with God reaps great rewards, but unlike earthly rewards, ours are eternal. He who dies with the most toys still dies, but he who invests with God reaps eternal rewards. It's the only truly stable financial investment.

chapter 8

"All of us interpret the world around us, and we tend toward seeing the world, and our life, in largely positive or negative terms."
–Martin Selgiman, psychologist.

Two friends, one an optimist and the other a pessimist, could never agree on a topic of discussion. The optimist being frustrated with the pessimist thought of a way to get his friend to think optimistically. The optimist amazingly had a dog that could walk on water, so he took the pessimist out hunting on the lake with his dog. He was rewarded quickly with a duck that splashed into the water a ways away from the boat. The dog jumped out of the boat, ran across the top of the water, grabbed the duck, and started to run back. The optimist looked over at the pessimist and asked what he thought about the dog. The pessimist looked at the dog and replied, "That dog can't swim, can he?"

What is the chief difference between a pessimist and an optimist? It falls on what things you think are universal and what things you think are specific to the situation. A pessimist sees negative things as being universal–"Diets never work." A pessimist also sees positive things not as being universal, but as being specific to the situation–"I lost some weight, but I'll probably gain it back." An optimist is the opposite. They see negative things as specific to the situation–"I messed up on my diet, but it was just because of the holiday." They also see positive things as universals–"This diet really works."

For thousands of years, the debate between optimism and pessimism has raged. As you're reading this, you're probably categorizing yourself and thinking about how you view the world around you. Some people claim there's a third group–the "realist." I was once one of those people. A realist says that they are neither a pessimist nor an optimist. They don't expect the worse like a pessimist or expect the best like the optimist. Their expected outcome is correct because that's just the way things always happen. As a realist, I gave my expected outcome to others, and I was always categorized by the listeners as a pessimist. Why was that? It's because a realist hides behind a different term, so he doesn't appear like a pessimist, but the realist is actually a pessimist in disguise.

A pessimist, an optimist, and an engineer were all sitting down at dinner in a nice restaurant one night, when all of the sudden, the pessimist noticed his glass was half empty. He said, "I've got to get a refill because my glass is half empty." The optimist corrected him and said, "Don't you mean it's half full?" Well, the debate started and became heated until they both turned to the engineer to seek his opinion. The engineer looked down at the glass and said, "Who's the moron that made that glass? It holds two times the volume that it needs to hold!" As funny as this is, the glass was once full. I'm sorry to say that there's only two groups. You either have a positive outlook on life or a negative one. There is no gray area in the middle; there's a dividing line. You decide which side you're on.

So what? What does it matter if you're a pessimist or an optimist. Does it really matter in life? Are both needed to balance out the earth? Well, it matters to God. Christ told us in John 15:10-11, "If ye keep my commandments, ye shall abide in my love; even as I have kept my Father's commandments, and abide in his love. These things have I spoken unto you, that my joy might remain in you, and that your joy might be full." It's important to God that our joy is full.

When I first started to work for the church, my pastor graciously invited me to go to Cedar Point theme park in Ohio, free of charge. We drove down early that Thursday morning and got in the park. I began to ride the rides and noticed something familiar. I had been on all these rides in some way or another at one of the eight theme parks I had been to in California growing up. Although these rides were all found in one park in Ohio, they weren't as big as the ones found in the multiple parks in California. For instance, there's a ride at Cedar Point called Power Tower that is two hundred feet tall. That same ride at Knott's Berry Farm in California is three hundred feet tall. I began to compare all the rides, and my negativity came out. I met up with Pastor Ouellette later that day, and he asked me how I liked it. I told him my new found truth of how California's rides were better. I later realized how much of a *jerk* I was! Here, my pastor had been so kind to provide a ride for me to the theme park and pay for my ticket, and I had the audacity to find something wrong with it. In that same passage of John 15, Christ commands us to love one another. I Corinthians told me that true love is kind, it isn't puffed up, and it thinketh no evil. I failed on three counts! No wonder Christ's joy wasn't in me. I didn't keep His commandments. I had the opportunity to enjoy the whole day, but my outlook was skewed. I dwelt on the negative, and it led me down a path that I regret.

The pessimists and optimists both follow a pattern, but their ends are amazingly different. I've listed those patterns below:

Pessimist	Optimist
1. Unthankful with what is presented	1. Gratitude with what is presented
2. Discontentment	2. Contentment
3. Lack of enthusiasm	3. Enthusiastic outlook
4. Views infect others	4. Views encourage others
5. Alienates himself	5. Instills endearment of himself to others
6. Devastates from within and decreases productivity	6. Looks to the future and increases productivity

Let's incorporate these patterns into a real life event. Let's take the pessimist first and put him in a church service. The pastor gets up and is excited to announce the church's drama they will be performing this year. The pessimist sits there and doesn't stop to think that a lot of churches don't do stuff like this and are dead. He immediately jumps to discontentment. He doesn't know why the church has to always do these things. He then thinks, "I hope the drama is not dorky like last years," or "I'll probably get rejected by someone I invite." He begins to grumble to those he knows, and they begin to think the same way and lose interest. These people that he knows are now reminded that they don't like hanging around this guy because he's always negative. The people of the church don't invite anyone, the choir doesn't sing with enthusiasm, and the drama is a total mess, which reinforces the pessimist's views about it. He is a self-fulfilling prophecy. It's his fault there wasn't any productivity in the whole event. Now, take the optimist and put him in the same situation. He's happy his church is moving forward and active. He's content with the pastor's direction, and is excited about the drama. He begins to think of all those he could invite and shares his prayer requests with friends. They too begin to think of others also, and the enthusiasm is spreading. People like to be around this guy because this guy has a good outlook and is fun to be around. The visitors come, the people work hard, and the drama is a success. The optimist is excited about the next year, and the church moves forward.

The patterns and the stories of my failures as a pessimist can go as a warning, but what is God's perspective? What are some spiritual reasons to have an optimistic view and therefore be joyful? Think about this–God's greatest joy, as found in Hebrews 12, was that He died on the cross, so that we might be saved. Our chief Example of a perfect life found joy, while being beaten by men; while a crown of thorns was smashed into His head; while men whipped him over and over and over; while having his robe stripped from his bloody body, the cloth pulling at his wounds; while carrying a cross up a hill; while hearing His own people mock and condemn Him; while having stakes smashed through his hands; while being dropped, cross and all, into an upright position; while his previously torn back had to rub up and down against a piece of rough wood so He could get breath; while His Father turned His back on Him; and while he bore our sins on the cross. He found joy in all that because of what he was doing for us. All that, and we struggle finding joy in the good things.

The welfare and joy of God's saints is extremely important. Philippians 1:27 says, "Only let your conversation be as it becometh the gospel of Christ: that whether I come and see you, or else be absent, I may hear of your affairs, that ye stand fast in one spirit, with one mind striving together for the faith of the gospel;" In chapter two verse two, Paul says, "Fulfil ye my joy, that ye be likeminded, having the same love, being of one accord, of one mind." How can a church move forward and do great things for God if there are pessimists in the congregation. The Bible says we are to mark those who cause division in the church. Do you want to be one of those marked people?

The Bible also makes 155 references to the word "joy." Below, you can see what God says about joy in a few of these verses. Take the time to think about them.

Ps 5:11 But let all those that put their trust in thee rejoice: let them ever shout for joy, because thou defendest them: let them also that love thy name be joyful in thee.
Ps 16:11 Thou wilt shew me the path of life: in thy presence is fulness of joy; at thy right hand there are pleasures for evermore.
Ps 27:6 And now shall mine head be lifted up above mine enemies round about me: therefore will I offer in his tabernacle sacrifices of joy; I will sing, yea, I will sing praises unto the LORD.
Ps 30:5 For his anger endureth but a moment; in his favour is life: weeping may endure for a night, but joy cometh in the morning.
Ps 32:11 Be glad in the LORD, and rejoice, ye righteous: and shout for joy, all ye that are upright in heart.
Pr 17:21 He that begetteth a fool doeth it to his sorrow: and the father of a fool hath no joy.
Pr 21:15 It is joy to the just to do judgment: but destruction shall be to the workers of iniquity.
Pr 23:24 The father of the righteous shall greatly rejoice: and he that begetteth a wise child shall have joy of him.
Mt 2:10 When they saw the star, they rejoiced with exceeding great joy.
Lu 6:23 Rejoice ye in that day, and leap for joy: for, behold, your reward is great in heaven: for in the like manner did their fathers unto the prophets.
Lu 15:7 I say unto you, that likewise joy shall be in heaven over one sinner that repenteth, more than over ninety and nine just persons, which need no repentance.
Ro 15:13 Now the God of hope fill you with all joy and peace in believing, that ye may abound in hope, through the power of the Holy Ghost.
1Th 2:19 For what is our hope, or joy, or crown of rejoicing? Are not even ye in the presence of our Lord Jesus Christ at his coming?

We have so many spiritual things to think on that can bring us joy. We've seen God's perspective about optimism, but what about a secular perspective? How do doctors view the differences between optimism and pessimism? The December 2006 issue of the medical journal Mayo Clinic Proceedings published the results of a medical experiment. In the mid-1960s, researchers administered personality tests to more than 7,000 students at the University of North Carolina at Chapel Hill. The test separated the students into two groups, the pessimists being the greater group. The researchers tracked the students for the next forty years and found that pessimists were 42% more likely to die from any cause than the optimists. The death rate was 42% higher in pessimists. Charles S. Carver,

Ph.D, a psychology professor at the University of Miami, studied these results and said there are two reasons for the great difference. First, optimists tend to take better care of themselves, usually in diet and exercise. Second, pessimists worry too much and are prone to medical problems due to stress and anxiety, the chief medical problem being heart disease. Another study showed that optimists have lower rates of depression, catch fewer infectious diseases, have stronger immune systems, and respond better to cancer treatments.

Also, ask the Wright brothers what they think about optimism. Ask the critics that for years said man couldn't fly what they think about pessimism. Who are these critics? Do you know their names? What about the critics that said man couldn't break the sound barrier? Chuck Yeager and the engineers at Bell Aircraft had a different opinion. Want to ask Roger Banister what he thought about the pessimists that said he couldn't run a mile in four minutes? History doesn't remember the pessimists. It remembers the optimists that push past adversity and fulfill their own prophecy.

So, what do you do if you're a pessimist? How do you break the cycle? I'm telling you, it's not easy to do. I struggled with it, and I still do on occasion, but there are ways.

First, in any situation, no matter if it is good or bad, think of three good things about it. For example, imagine you get in a car accident. #1 You're alive! #2 You got to use that car for all that time up to the accident! #3 You're alive! There's always positives. There's a chance to witness to the other driver. You still are going to heaven some day in the future. You can find so much good in life.

Second, when tough times come or you feel depressed, give to others. Christ found joy in giving to us even in a tough time. You'll find so much joy in dwelling on others that you will forget yourself.

Third, pray for others. Just like giving, when you pray for others, you tend to see others that have it worse than you do, and your heart is focused on the things that God is focused on.

Fourth, respond agreeably to criticism. I have some friends that you cannot put down. They beat you to it. I can approach them and say, "You've got a weight problem," and they'll say, "You're telling me! Even Jenny Craig won't accept me." It will take the fire out of any attack because there's no where to go. They don't really think they're fat, but they divert it to a joke.

Fifth, always look to what God has done for you and count your blessings. Just like the song says, you can "name them one by one, and you will be surprised at what the Lord has done."

As said before, joy is extremely vital to your spiritual life, to those around you, and to your health. It's not something to be taken lightly. A mature man will realize there's so much more to life than the expected doom of a situation. Be joyful.

work ethic
fundamentals for every day life

chapter 9

"The idle man does not know what it is to enjoy rest."
–Albert Einstein

Upon telling a friend of mine that I'm not able to do something because I have to work, he often replies, "Work is overrated." It produces a laugh in me every time. My friend is not lazy at all. He's one of the hardest workers I know. I often think it would be nice to retire, but not so I wouldn't have to work, but because I will have enough time for the work that I want to do. I've always wanted to build an airplane and a boat (not at the same time). I also enjoy helping out at the church which I attend. I enjoy working, but for some reason when my alarm clock goes off at 4:30 in the morning, my first thought is "I don't want to go to work." I'd rather be sleeping, waking when I want to wake up, and doing the work I want to do. Do you ever feel the same way? If you're reading this book, you either attend school or work a job (or hope to), so I imagine I've hit a nerve with you. Very few people are morning people. Are you one of those? It's easy to stay up late, but it's hard to wake up early.

Lack of sleep isn't the only downfall of having to work. We also have to do things we don't want to. I love my job at 9-1-1, but amazingly,

I don't like to answer phones. I like when I could just sit there and read my Bible, or talk to co-workers, or work on a puzzle of some sort. But, then the phone rings, and I'm interrupted! What are these people thinking calling 9-1-1? Don't they have something better to do? Think of a task or job you don't like to do. Do you not like washing dishes? Do you not like working on the car, making the bed, studying, etc. You name it. There are many tasks that we don't like to do, and some tasks we think are hard. Several of my coworkers complain because the work environment isn't up to their par. They want better chairs to sit on and longer breaks. As tough as our work seems, we don't have it too badly. Below is a notice that was found in some ruins in an old London office building. The notice was dated 1852:

> *1. This firm has reduced the hours of work, and the clerical staff will now only have to be present between the hours of 7 a.m. and 6 p.m. weekdays.*
> *2. Clothing must be of a sober nature. The clerical staff will not disport themselves in raiment of bright colors, nor will they wear hose unless in good repair.*
> *3. Overshoes and topcoats may not be worn in the office, but neck scarves and headwear may be worn in inclement weather.*
> *4. A stove is provided for the benefit of the clerical staff. Coal and wood must be kept in the locker. It is recommended that each member of the clerical staff bring four pounds of coal each day during the cold weather.*
> *5. No member of the clerical staff may leave the room without permission from the supervisor.*
> *6. No talking is allowed during business hours.*
> *7. The craving for tobacco, wine, or spirits is a human weakness, and as such is forbidden to all members of the clerical staff.*
> *8. Now that the hours of business have been drastically reduced, the partaking of food is allowed between 11:30 and noon, but work will not on any account cease.*
> *9. Members of the clerical staff will provide their own pens. A new sharpener is available on application to the supervisor.*
> *10. The supervisor will nominate a senior clerk to be responsible for the cleanliness of the main office and the private office. All boys and juniors will report to him 40 minutes before prayers and will remain after closing hours for similar work. Brushes, brooms, scrubber, and soap are provided by the owners.*
> *11. The owners recognize the generosity of the new labor laws, but will expect a great rise in output of work to compensate for these near Utopian conditions.*

That's a tough work environment that the supervision thought to be

"Utopian." What do you mean that I have to bring my own coal, provide my own pens, and have no breaks??? That company would have been sued in modern days. People actually worked in these environments and were thankful to have jobs. Was the notice too far removed for you? Visit a farm sometime and help out. Wake up before dawn to feed the animals and milk the cows. Then, do your ten other chores for the morning and have breakfast. Clean up, and you're either off to school or off to do more work on the farm (depending on your age). We don't really have it that tough. I remember my mom nagging me to put the dishes in the dishwasher, not clean my own dishes, just stick them in the dishwasher. What a hard task! Yet, I couldn't bring myself to exert such energy. We all have our tasks that we despise, and we all have various beliefs on how to work, but what are God's thoughts on work? What is His definition of a good work ethic?

First, God never intended for work to be a punishment. As much as we don't like various tasks, work is not supposed to be a punishment. Genesis 2:15 accounts God's purpose for Adam in the Garden of Eden, "And the LORD God took the man, and put him into the garden of Eden to dress it and to keep it." Adam was supposed to work the garden. In the same chapter, he had to give names to all the animals. This was a perfect environment. It wasn't till chapter three that you find sin entering the garden. Why would man be punished for not doing anything wrong yet? God never saw work as a punishment.

When I was twelve, my dad got this great idea of taking me to work with him during the summer months. My mom worked and couldn't watch me, so I went to the construction sites with my dad. I remember many mornings, waking up at 4:30 AM, leaving the house at 5:00 AM, driving two hours to the job site, working twelve hours till 7:00 PM, then driving two hours back home arriving at 9:00 PM, then going to sleep, so I could wake up the next morning and do it all over again. I didn't understand why I couldn't stay at home. I didn't get much sleep for a summer "vacation." I had to work in the summer heat painting houses, carrying loads of equipment, cleaning equipment, etc. My friends were staying home, playing video games, and having a good time. Not me. I was stuck doing manual labor. You ask my dad why he did it, and he'll give you a bunch of reasons including, "I wanted him to see what manual labor was like, so he would get an office job," or "I didn't want him at home getting in trouble," or "I wanted to teach him a trade." Well, they all worked. I look back on those years and am so thankful for them. When school would come around, waking up at 6:30 AM and then studying that evening was a vacation compared to working with my dad. I loved school. I never got in trouble during the summer while working with my dad, and I learned many valuable skills that have helped me in my marriage. I was able to incorporate them the week after my wife and I got home from our honeymoon. We found mold in an exterior wall and I had to replace it in the middle of winter. I owe all the ability to my dad and his training. Work is not a punishment.

Work is a means to provide food for yourself. Proverbs 12:11 says, "He that tilleth his land shall be satisfied with bread: but he that followeth vain persons is void of understanding." He also says in II Thessalonians 3:10 that if you don't work, you don't eat. My parents provided so much for me. My mom cooked meals that I ate, and my parents bought me clothing that I wore, sent me to a private school, and occasionally paid for something entertaining. I didn't do anything to deserve it. They worked for me. I regret not pitching in more around the house. I could have helped provide for myself. Work is a way of providing for yourself.

Not only is it a way of providing for yourself, it's a way of providing for others. My wife and I are blessed with good jobs, and we don't live outside of our means. On occasion, we like to provide things for others who don't have the same means we do. We both like to give more than we like to receive. We feel awkward getting things from people, but we really enjoy secretly giving to people and then hearing their stories of how it was a blessing. I also enjoy providing for my wife. I love to see her face light up when I bring home flowers for no special occasion–just because I love her. I Timothy 5:8 says, "But if any provide not for his own, and specially for those of his own house, he hath denied the faith, and is worse than an infidel." An infidel is a person who has no faith or whose faith is very weak. God says your faith in Him and in His Word is nothing if you do not provide for your family. That's a pretty strong passage. It makes sense. God commands us to love our wives and to love others. The greatest love is a giving love. If we don't give or provide for our family, then we aren't loving and therefore aren't trusting that God's way is best.

Working is also a path to greater. In 1901, the company founded by Andrew Carnegie was taken over by U.S. Steel Corporation. Along with taking over the company, they had to honor the salary of the top executive, Charles M. Schwab (ever heard of the name?). The contract stated that they had to pay him $1,000,000. The top salary on record at that time was $100,000. J.P. Morgan confronted Charles Schwab and asked him what could be done about it. Charles took the contract and tore it up. He later told Forbes magazine, "I didn't care what salary they paid me. I was not animated by money motives. I believed in what I was trying to do, and I wanted to see it brought about. I canceled the contract without a moment's hesitation. Why do I work? I work for just the pleasure I find in work, the satisfaction there is in developing things, in creating. Also, the associations business begets. The person who does not work for the love of work, but only for money, is not likely to make money nor to find much fun in life." This man's name still lives today as one of the top investing firms in the world. He cut his own salary because it wasn't important to him. He found satisfaction in developing things. Have you ever built something? The completion of it is a wonderful experience. It's not a huge work all at one time; it's the little things you do each day that progresses you to the end. Luke 16:10 says, "He that is faithful in that which is least is faithful also in much: and he that is unjust in the least is unjust also in much." God says the path to greater things is found in the small things you do on a daily basis. So, how do you do these small things?

God has His views on how to work also. He doesn't just tell us to work, He gives us many different ways to work, so that we will be proficient. He tells us that we are to work as if we're working for Him.

"And whatsoever ye do, do it heartily, as to the Lord, and not unto men" (Col. 3:23). God sees us all the time and is watching how we work. A story was told by Howard A. Stein in a *Readers Digest* about a friend of his that retired and "became interested in the construction of an addtion to a shopping mall. Observing the activity regularly, he was especially impressed by the conscientious operator of a large piece of equipment. The day finally came when my friend had a chance to tell this man how much he'd enjoyed watching his scrupulous work. Looking astonished, the operator replied, 'You're not the supervisor?'" The construction operator was meticulously working because he thought this man that was watching him was his boss. We have to keep in mind that God is watching us 24/7, 365 days-a-year, and we are to work heartily for him.

Ecclesiastes 9:10 says, "Whatsoever thy hand findeth to do, do it with thy might; for there is no work, nor device, nor knowledge, nor wisdom, in the grave, whither thou goest." We are to strive for excellence in all that we do. I often think that churches get too involved with "what can we do," instead of "what should we do and how should we do it." I've never been impressed with poor workmanship. Many times people focus on doing several things and just getting things done, but rarely do they actually put forth a good effort to provide a high-quality production. Likewise, the "big box stores" that have popped up in the last few decades are very convenient. They have everything you want all in one store for a good price, but have you ever brought the stuff home and thought it was the cheapest junk you've ever bought? In the same regards, market yourself and the things you do. Would a company that really knows you want to hire you? Do you strive for excellence in all that you do? God says we are supposed to do whatever we do to the best of our ability.

Not only are we supposed to be quality workers, we're supposed to work as if the end is coming. I John 9:4 says, "I must work the works of him that sent me, while it is day: the night cometh, when no man can work." The reason why my dad woke up so early is because he wanted to do all he could while light was out. Once the sun went down, it was hard to paint houses. "Whereas ye know not what shall be on the morrow. For what is your life? It is even a vapour, that appeareth for a little time, and then vanisheth away" (James 4:14). Your life is going to fly by. Will you look back and wish you had done things differently or worked harder?

Through this whole chapter, all you've heard is "work, work, work!" Are you shocked? It's what the chapter of the book said. Well, here's the good news: God didn't just tell us how to work; He told us how to rest also. "Six days thou shalt do thy work, and on the seventh day thou shalt rest: that thine ox and thine ass may rest, and the son of thy handmaid, and the stranger, may be refreshed" (Exodus 23:12). You have to rest at least one day a week. The reason why–so you can get refreshed to do more work. Don't disregard this warning. If God needs a day to rest, you definitely need one, too.

So, with all this work, what are the benefits of a good work ethic? We've already seen that promotion comes by a good work ethic. Why would God give you great things if you don't take care of the little things?

Another benefit can be found in the story of Joseph. God gave him the dream that said there would be seven years of plenty and seven years of famine. Joseph led the people to work hard the first seven years and build up their storehouses. That food not only lasted them through the seven years of famine, it was sold to people in many countries to make much money. Proverbs 10:4 says, "He becometh poor that dealeth with a slack hand: but the hand of the diligent maketh rich." With a good work ethic, you'll have provision in not only the bad times but in the good also.

Proverbs 13:4 says, "The soul of the sluggard desireth, and hath nothing: but the soul of the diligent shall be made fat." Having a good work ethic is good for your soul. I enjoy building things. I drew up some plans for two different queen size beds in my house and then began working on them. It took many long hours of work, but when I walk through my house now, the sight of the beds brings me enjoyment. They were a completion of an arduous process, and they are the way I wanted them. God looked at his creation and numerous times said it was good. Hard work (and the product of it) is good for your soul.

God has commanded us to have a good work ethic, He's told us how to do it, and He's given us benefits for it. If you follow these patterns in becoming a man God's way, you'll attain joy from the fruits of your labor.

chapter 10

"Communication works for those who work at it."
–John Powell

The average woman speaks over 25,000 words a day. The average man speaks only 10,000 words. Men don't convey their thoughts the same way, and they don't share their thoughts as much. Men don't always convey thoughts with enough description, or we convey it in description that's over the other person's head. For instance, I could say "I saw those varmints run and chase her till she chopped their tail," and you might not get what I was talking about, even though it made sense in my head. How about this, "Three myopic rodents. Three myopic rodents. Observe how they perambulate. Observe how they perambulate. They all circumnavigated the agriculturist's significant other, who amputated their extremities with a carving utensil. Did you ever observe such an occurrence in your existence as three myopic rodents?" Okay . . . that's a little over people's heads. I went overboard in explaining what happened. So what am I actually talking about? "Three blind mice. Three blind mice. See how they run. See how they run. They all ran after the farmer's wife who cut off their tails with a carving knife. Did you ever see such a sight in your life, as three blind mice?"

Communication is not an easy thing for men, and many of us take it for granted. As frustrated as we get with women's incessant speech, communication is very important. We often look at it as inconsequential. We think that words are just words. We see them as a hassle and a waste of time. Is there any significance to our use of words? Do they really matter? Well, let me ask you–do you recognize any of these phrases:

> *"Religion is the sigh of the oppressed creature, the heart of a heartless world, and the soul of soulless conditions. It is the opium of the people."*
> –Karl Mark (beliefs led to communism)

> *"I do not see why man should not be just as cruel as nature"*
> –Adolph Hitler (Holocaust leader)

> *"Mr Gorbachev, tear down this wall!"*
> –Ronald Reagan (Brought an end to the Cold War)

> *"I have a dream that my four little children will one day live in a nation where they will not be judged by the color of their skin, but by the content of their character."*
> –Martin Luther King, Jr. (Led to bring about civil rights)

These are just short statements, but they've reverberated down through our recent history, and they mean a great amount to many people.

Words are very powerful. God could have waved His hand to create the whole universe, but He chose to speak it into existence. He said, "Let there be light," and there was light that still shines today. A sun came into existence that is 109 times as large as the earth. But, that's just our sun. Look up into the heavens at night and behold the stars in their vast number. They were all created by His spoken word, each one a sun or a planet.

God's words are powerful, and in giving us His words, He tells us that our words are powerful, too. James 3:1-8:

> *1 My brethren, be not many masters, knowing that we shall receive the greater condemnation.*
> *2 For in many things we offend all. If any man offend not in word, the same is a perfect man, and able also to bridle the whole body.*
> *3 Behold, we put bits in the horses' mouths, that they may obey us; and we turn about their whole body.*
> *4 Behold also the ships, which though they be so great, and are driven of fierce winds, yet are they turned about with a very small helm, whithersoever the governor listeth.*
> *5 Even so the tongue is a little member, and boasteth great things. Behold, how great a matter a little fire kindleth!*
> *6 And the tongue is a fire, a world of iniquity: so is the tongue among our members, that it defileth the whole body, and setteth on fire the course of nature; and it is set on fire of hell.*
> *7 For every kind of beasts, and of birds, and of serpents, and of things in the sea, is tamed, and hath been tamed of mankind:*
> *8 But the tongue can no man tame; it is an unruly evil, full of deadly poison.*

God warns us that the tongue, as small as it is, "setteth on fire the course of nature." Earlier we read those quotes from famous people, and their words brought great change, or destruction, or building to our world. With a few simple words, I can either make my wife fall in love with me again, or I can alienate her for the rest of my life. God says that if you are able to tame your tongue, you're a perfect man, but then He says later that no man can tame the tongue. God isn't telling us to give up. He's telling us that it is going to be our biggest battle, and we will have failures. We need to do our best as men to have good communication. To do that, we need to understand how it works.

Your speech does not begin at your mouth. It does not begin at your brain. Your speech begins at your heart. Matthew 12:34-35 says, "O generation of vipers, how can ye, being evil, speak good things? for out of the abundance of the heart the mouth speaketh. A good man out of the good treasure of the heart bringeth forth good things: and an evil man out of the evil treasure bringeth forth evil things." Whatever is in your heart will proceed out of your mouth. If your heart is wicked or if your heart is harboring sin, your mouth will speak of such wickedness. If I'm feeling selfish, if I'm not doing my Bible reading, if I'm harboring any sin in my heart, my speech toward others will betray any outward persona I have. My wife knows when I'm spiritually struggling as I know when she is. Her speech proclaims her heart's welfare. Often times I don't want to talk to my wife. Some occasions might be a football game or a project on which I'm working. She'll start to talk to me, and my annoyance meter begins to rise. Guess what? It's not her fault. It's mine. I have a problem with my heart. You see, I want to watch the game. I want to work on the project. I don't want to listen. Did you notice all the "I's"? I have a problem with selfishness and a lack of love. At the core of bad communication is a problem of the heart.

So what? What does it matter? Are there really dangers if I don't communicate well? Matthew 12:36-37 says, "But I say unto you, That every idle word that men shall speak, they shall give account thereof in the day of judgment. For by thy words thou shalt be justified, and by thy words thou shalt be condemned." That sounds like it matters a great deal. Once words leave our mouths, they travel in all directions at a speed of around 770 miles per hour and you can't get the words back. They've left my mouth. If I have bad communication, I will have to give account of it one day. God warns us in Ecclesiastes 5:2, "Be not rash with thy mouth, and let not thine heart be hasty to utter any thing before God: for God is in heaven, and thou upon earth: therefore let thy words be few." Our hearts are wicked and our speech proceeds from our hearts. We can work on our hearts, but God's backup plan is not to speak without thinking.

Not only are we responsible for the bad things we say, we are responsible for what we say in general. That verse in Matthew that is listed above doesn't say "bad word"; it says "idle word." Many times I think my thoughts are heard. I'll be thinking about something and tell my wife. She will ask me a question about the same thing that I've already gone over in my head, and I'll bite her head off for not understanding. Sometimes, I'll try to explain something to her, and she won't understand my terminology. For instance, I'll be working on a project and ask her to go get me a 3/8 inch open-ended wrench. She gives me a blank stare as if I asked her to realign the photon emitters on the space ship's phaser arrays. I could see the wheels turning in her head as she dissects each word, "3/8 inch--okay that's the size, open ended–have no clue what that means, wrench–aha! pliers." She goes off for a little while and comes back with twenty tools, none of which are correct. Whose fault is it? Mine. I didn't train her or give her the words she could understand. My communication was faulty. After a couple of requests like that, she's frustrated, and I'm going to be sleeping on the couch.

There are some keyss we need to remember about our communication that will help us. The first key is that people aren't mind readers. They don't know what you're thinking. Cecil B. DeMille was a famous movie maker. On one occasion, he set up six cameras to pick up all the action of the scene he was shooting. The cast started rehearsing at six in the morning and kept rehearsing till late in the afternoon. The sun began to set, and Cecil saw that the setting was perfect. He gave the command for action, and the hundred extras charged up the hill and another hundred came down. They clashed in fight, while others depicting Roman centurions yelled at two hundred slaves who worked to move a large stone. The lines that had been rehearsed where being said in closeup to the cameras as fifteen minutes went by. Cecil liked what he saw and yelled, "Cut!" He was so pleased. People were telling him it looked great. He looked and waved to the camera crew on top of the hill to see if they got all of it okay, and the camera supervisor waved back, raised his megaphone, and yelled, "Ready when you are, C.B.!" All of that work and waiting for nothing. Why? Lack of communication. Cecil's thoughts were not heard.

Another key to communication we need to remember is that people don't have the same knowledge you have. I grew up in a family that did construction, art, missions work, sports, etc. Out of those, my wife has only been involved in sports. I have to expound on things with which she's not familiar. Remember that people didn't have the same background you did. Your life has brought you to where you are now and has led a unique path that no one completely understands. You have to take that into account when communicating.

Also, remember that people are not perfect. They are going to get frustrated and react if things aren't going well. They are going to take the things you say in a wrong way. They are going to judge you for how you say things and what you say. You are the only person responsible for your speech. They are going to misunderstand what you're trying to say. When J. Edgar Hoover took over the FBI, everyone wanted to impress him. One young man decided it would impress Mr. Hoover if he saved money by reducing the size of the office memo paper. Hoover saw it on his desk and immediately didn't like it. He wrote on it, "Watch the borders!" and sent it back. For the next six weeks, travelers found it extremely difficult to cross over the Mexican or Canadian borders. Remember to be patient with people. As the verse in Ecclesiastes says, "Be not rash with thy mouth."

Another key to remember is that it's much harder to rebuild something than it is to tear it down. The World Trade Center took five years to complete. It took a couple of hours to bring it down. Your speech (and reputation) can take years to build, but seconds to bring it down. If you use your communication to gossip, complain, etc., you're tearing down things that may have taken years to build. It's much harder to rebuild what's been torn down.

We've discussed that your speech is a powerful thing, and there's many things to keep in mind about communication, but how do you progress to good communication? Besides the things already mentioned, you can learn to listen. This helps with the "not speaking rashly" part. If you talk less and listen more, you'll be surprised at how much you learn and how much you don't get in trouble. One of my biggest pet peeves is when you're listening to something and the person next to you doesn't quite get what was just said, so they ask you what was said. Now, you have to explain to them what was just said and try to listen at the same time.

Usually, if the person just listens longer instead of asking, they hear it again or they hear a follow up to it that explains it.

Also, you can ask more questions, and offer less information about yourself or your topics. People like to talk about themselves, but rarely like to hear about another person. You'll make friends if you ask questions about them in a conversation. Often times, the other person feels fulfilled in being able to talk about themselves. They get bored with themselves and start asking you questions. They're now ready to listen, and they think highly of you, because during your conversation, you showed interest in them, and that is a friendly trait.

Another thing you can do is to put the conversation on the bottom shelf. People don't care if you know fancy words. I hate not knowing what a word means, and it further irritates me when someone is trying to show off by using it. You don't want to lose a listener with fancy words. They are in the conversation not to hear your eloquence; they are there to receive and give information. In addition, always take time to make sure your wording is understood. Follow up on it, and don't treat the person like they are dumb for not understanding.

You will have to give account for all you say, and communication is extremely hard to master. Keep your heart from evil, think before you speak, and remember where people are coming from, and your communication will be free from many problems.

conclusion
now the work begins

"That's all folks!"
–Mel Blanc

In becoming a man God's way, you have to redefine your thinking. You have to disregard what society has told you about manliness, love, security, faith, leadership, purity, finances, joyfulness, working, and communication, and you have to rebuild your foundation through God.

The chapters you just read are not all-inclusive. They aren't all you need. They are just a guide to get you on the right foot. They were meant to get you to think about your actions and move you forward. If you want a complete guide, read your Bible. The Bible is complete and perfect, and if you don't depart from it, it will bring you success in life. Take time each day to let the mirror of God's word show you who you really are and show you Who you should be like. The Bible is God's roadmap to *Becoming a Man . . . God's Way.*

www.ingramcontent.com/pod-product-compliance
Lightning Source LLC
LaVergne TN
LVHW091314080426
835510LV00007B/497